cooking for Jeffrey

cooking for Jeffrey

a barefoot contessa cookbook

ina garten

Photographs by Quentin Bacon

Garden photographs by John M. Hall

CLARKSON POTTER/PUBLISHERS

New York

Copyright © 2016 by Ina Garten

All rights reserved.
Published in the United States by Clarkson Potter/
Publishers, an imprint of the Crown Publishing Group,
a division of Penguin Random House LLC, New York.
crownpublishing.com
clarksonpotter.com

CLARKSON POTTER is a trademark and POTTER with
colophon is a registered trademark of
Penguin Random House LLC.

Library of Congress Cataloging-in-Publication Data
is available upon request.

ISBN 978-0-307-46489-7
Ebook ISBN 978-0-8041-8703-9

Printed in Hong Kong

Design by Marysarah Quinn
Photographs by Quentin Bacon
Garden photographs copyright © 2016 by John M. Hall
Photographs on pages 3, 12, 14, 15, 20, 45, and 132 are
from the author's collection.

10 9 8 7 6 5 4 3 2 1

First Edition

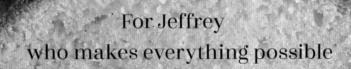

For Jeffrey
who makes everything possible

contents

thank you!

Writing a cookbook is like creating a great ballet; it's a collaboration between choreographers and dancers, and that's actually the pleasure of it—creating something together that you all love doing. I work with so many people whom I love and admire.

First and foremost is my team, starting with Barbara Libath, who has worked side by side with me since the first book in 1999. She is my dear friend and we do everything together, including testing every recipe in every book to make sure they will work for you at home. If we cook something together during the day and she goes home and makes it for her family that night, I know it's a winner.

Lidey Heuck joined us three years ago and Barbara and I can't imagine life without her. As Barbara has become such an accomplished cook, we now watch Lidey prepare each recipe to see what things a twenty-something might find challenging. We are a happy band of coconspirators and every day is fun. Work just doesn't get any better than this!

My team at Penguin Random House/Crown/Clarkson Potter and I have been together since 1999 when they first published *The Barefoot Contessa Cookbook*. They took a chance on an unknown author, gave me the freedom to fly, and always supported me. Maya Mavjee, David Drake, Aaron Wehner, Kate Tyler, Rica Allannic, and most of all, my amazing editor, Pam Krauss, and my brilliant book designer, Marysarah Quinn, who make me look so much better than I am! Thank you for providing such a happy place for me to be with a group of extraordinary people!

I have photographed so many books with the same team—the brilliant Quentin Bacon takes the most gorgeous photographs, Cyd McDowell and Vivian Lui prepare the most beautiful food, and Barb Fritz brings us gorgeous dishes to put it all on. I love every day that we work together. I also love working with John Hall, who takes beautiful photographs of my garden all year round.

Finally, thank you to my friend and agent Esther Newberg for taking care of business so I can do the fun stuff. And thank you, too, to my wonderful friend Sarah Chase who always inspires me with new ideas for recipes. And, of course, the biggest thank-you is to my sweet husband, Jeffrey, who always makes me laugh and takes such good care of me. None of this would have happened without your love and inspiration.

camping trip Rome, 1971

intro

When I give talks I'm often asked what I make when I'm cooking just for myself. Truthfully, the answer is: not much! After all, I spend most of my days developing, testing, and retesting recipes for my cookbooks, so when dinner rolls around I'm very happy with a bowl of homemade soup or a tuna on rye from the deli. For me, cooking has always been as much about making people happy as it has been about satisfying a hunger pang. Cooking is more gratifying and, frankly, more fun when I'm cooking for people I love—whether for two friends or a party of twelve—and for more than forty years my most constant and appreciative audience has been my sweet husband, Jeffrey.

When I was growing up, I always wanted to cook but was never allowed in the kitchen. My mother used to say, "It's my job to cook and your job to study." I secretly think that my mother considered the kitchen her personal space, and she wasn't crazy about me making a mess or rearranging her pots and pans. So, the minute I married Jeffrey, I bought Craig Claiborne's *The New York Times Cookbook* and worked my way through the recipes until the book was coming apart at the seams. I made things Jeffrey loved: Spinach & Feta Strudel, Chili Con Carne, Shrimp Curry, along with lots of decadent desserts, like Chocolate Chiffon Pie and Crêpes Suzette. Though our tastes have certainly changed over the years, many of these early dishes have inspired the recipes in my cookbooks.

I loved the challenge of tackling a new dish, and the more complicated the recipe, the better! I remember one of the first things I tried was a braided challah (egg bread) for Friday-night dinner—not the easiest thing to make. All these years later I'm still making challah, but with my own, easier version of that recipe, Challah with Saffron (page 173). Working away in my own kitchen for the first time, I was in heaven, and I found mastering a difficult recipe and the creative part of cooking incredibly satisfying. Just as important to me, though, was that Jeffrey loved everything I cooked. His enthusiasm truly fueled the fire. I was making a home for us, which made me happy, and taking care of the love of my life.

It was Jeffrey who first encouraged me to turn what I considered more of a hobby or pastime into my career. When he and I had been married for less than a year, he came home one day and found me sitting on the sofa, watching *That Girl* on TV. (In case you don't remember the show,

Marlo Thomas played a young, independent working woman living on her own in New York City at a time when most single women that age were expected to live at home.) Jeffrey turned to me and said, "You need to do something with your life, or you'll never be happy." That stopped me short. I thought I was living the dream—I was married to the man I loved! But in time I realized he was right, and his words started me on a journey that has led to a life and happiness beyond any I could have imagined. I already loved to cook for Jeffrey, but he helped me realize I could do more with that interest. I often say that he was the first feminist I ever knew; he believed that I could do anything I wanted to do. He's the reason I love to cook and also the person who continually encourages me to do what I love.

It was Jeffrey who encouraged me to leave my job in government when I needed to find something more exciting and creative. He said, "Pick something you love to do. If you love it, you'll be really good at it." When I came across an ad for a little specialty food store in the Hamptons, I knew I'd found that thing. This was 1978, in an era when women were starting to work full-time and needed help getting dinner on the table. The idea of having a food store seemed like fun—I envisioned big platters of roast chickens and freshly baked cupcakes piled high, like having a big party every day with lots of good food, great music, and customers having a wonderful time. Running and operating Barefoot Contessa allowed me to share my love of food and cooking on a completely different scale. And Jeffrey was there again, nearly twenty years later, when I began to long for a new challenge and I made the decision to sell Barefoot Contessa to the manager and the chef.

The year that followed was the most difficult year of my life. I forced myself to go to my office every morning but ended up spending more than a few days reading magazines or copying over my address book. One morning, as Jeffrey was leaving to go to New Haven—he was now the dean of the business school at Yale and traveled back and forth between East Hampton and New Haven, Connecticut, every week—he asked me what I planned to do that week. Exasperated, I said, "Nothing! I have nothing to do all week!" Jeffrey smiled and gave me a great piece of advice. "You love the food business," he said. "Just stay in the game."

At exactly the same time, my friend Susan Newbold decided to change her professional life as well. Susan had been an interior designer in Santa Barbara, California, for decades and also felt it was time to shake things up. She had moved to Connecticut to be with her new husband, and since neither of us had anything to do, we spent lots of time trying to figure out what to do next.

I remember one day I said, "Let's figure out the parameters of what we want in our new jobs." We came up with four criteria. First, we decided that we wanted to have no employees. (Over the past twenty years, I had overseen between fifty and a hundred people a year and I didn't feel like solving anyone's boyfriend problems anymore!) Second, we wanted to do something that we were passionate about so our work didn't feel like "work." Third, of course, in order for it to be a business, we had to make a living doing it. And finally—and this was our private joke—we wanted businesses where we could drop everything at a moment's notice and go to Paris! At that point Susan and I would be doubled over with laughter—because, of course, that job didn't exist!!

Over the years, people had asked me to write a cookbook, but writing seemed so solitary, which was the opposite of what I had loved about the store. The store felt like a party and I was the hostess. Sitting at a computer all day didn't sound like all that much fun. But when you have absolutely nothing to do, having something to do—anything!—seems incredibly appealing, so instead of leafing through interior design magazines that day, I sat down and wrote a book proposal. The next day, I called the only agent I knew and asked if she would send my proposal to a top cookbook editor my friends Lee Bailey and Martha Stewart had recommended. I was certain it would go nowhere, but at least it kept me busy for a few days!

When the first publisher that saw it (and they remain my publisher to this day!) accepted my proposal, I was terrified but also thrilled, not only because I had finally found something to do but because at fifty years old I was beginning to worry that my professional life was behind me. What I couldn't have known then is that in some ways my career hadn't even started yet. Those early days of cooking for Jeffrey and my many years running a specialty food store were actually just preparation for what I've found to be my true passion—writing cookbooks.

Roast Chicken with Radishes (page 93)

When I look back at those days, I have to wonder if it's true that you can do anything that you can imagine. Susan Newbold became a successful artist. I work in a barn next to my home in East Hampton with two people I truly love; they are friends, not employees. I get up every morning and know that I get to do exactly what I want to do every day. And the best part is that, as Susan and I laughed about, she teaches art classes in France and Jeffrey and I go to Paris often. How great is that?

Cooking for Jeffrey is my tenth book, and I hope you'll enjoy it for the new recipes and because it's deeply personal. I've included many dishes that I have loved making for him over the years, as well as some inspired by the new ingredients and flavors I have discovered along the way. Many of the recipes I made during those early years I've updated for this book, such as Tarragon Shrimp Salad (page 82), Brisket with Onions and Leeks (page 96), Shrimp and Swordfish Curry (page 124), Fresh Corn Pancakes (page 150), and Fresh Peach Cobbler (page 235). Each one has been "Jeffrey-tested" again and again, but frankly, I'm not sure that means much, because Jeffrey seems to like everything I make for him, and that's exactly why I love to cook!

What *Cooking for Jeffrey* has taught me is the power of food. Cooking is one of the great gifts you can give to those you love. It says "you're important enough to me to spend the time and effort to cook for you."

There is nothing more comforting than walking into a house that smells like there's a roast chicken and onions or a homemade apple pie in the oven. And when people show up around your table, you create a community of friends who take care of each other, which is, for me, the whole point of cooking.

I think about this when I recall the last year of my dad's life. It was Thanksgiving and he was at a particularly wonderful assisted living home in New Canaan, Connecticut, called Waveny. As he wasn't totally lucid at that time, it would have been very difficult to bring him home for a Thanksgiving dinner, so instead, I made a Thanksgiving dinner and brought it to him. I invited everyone close to him—of course, my mom, who was living nearby, as well as the nurses and aides. I started with my best linens and flowers for the table and served up roast turkey and gravy, lots of stuffing, and all kinds of traditional side dishes. For dessert I brought his favorite pies and pumpkin mousse. I remember looking down that big table filled with delicious things to eat and so many people having a wonderful time in the middle of an assisted living home. My dad was sitting at the head of the table like the happy host, with a huge grin on his face. It was a wonderful sight. He exclaimed, "It's a party!" At this point in his life, I'm not sure he knew who we all were but he loved a party and he had a wonderful time that day. That's what I'll always remember.

*Challah with Saffron
(page 173)*

It doesn't really matter what the occasion is—big or small—but it's the connections that we have with people we love that nourish our souls. Entertaining isn't just about making dinner parties. It's about celebrating those connections and I think that's what makes life worth living.

I hope you and the people dearest to you love these recipes, too!

xxx's Ina

smoked salmon pizzas

aperol spritzer

perfect potato pancakes

limoncello vodka collins

smoked salmon pizzas

fried oysters with lemon saffron aioli

cocktails

french 75

dark rum southsides

butternut squash hummus

parmesan & chipotle popcorn

herbed fromage blanc

Jeffrey at Dartmouth

meeting Jeffrey

Jeffrey and I got off to a very rocky start and it involved cocktails—or more precisely, it didn't involve cocktails! Let me back up. When I was in high school in Connecticut, my parents and I spent one autumn weekend visiting my brother at Dartmouth College in Hanover, New Hampshire. Unbeknownst to me, Jeffrey and his roommate were in the college library studying as I walked by outside. Jeffrey just happened to look up at that moment. He asked his roommate, "Who's that girl?" (Dartmouth was an all-boys school then, so I'm sure any girl walking past would have caught his eye!) Amazingly, not only did I happen to know his roommate from our tennis club back home, but also my brother had arranged for me to have a date with him that night. His roommate replied, "Her name is Ina Rosenberg, and I'm taking her to the movies tonight."

The next day Jeffrey asked his roommate for my address. I received a beautiful handwritten letter in the mail (remember those days?) with a photograph of the most adorable guy I'd ever seen. A few months later he came to Connecticut and took me out on what turned out to be a totally disastrous date. I was sixteen and I tried to take him to a bar in a state where you couldn't drink until you were eighteen. I'd never actually been to a bar, but I figured that's where a college guy would expect to go, right? Unfortunately, I had no clue that I would need an ID to get past the bouncer at the door, let alone to be served. After we were summarily turned away at the door, we drove to a coffeehouse in Westport, Connecticut, and happily had a very good time. So much for impressing the college guy! Decades later, I asked Jeffrey why he wanted to see me again after that mortifying first date and he said, "I decided you needed taking care of." Be still my heart.

aperol spritzer

makes 6 drinks

Aperol is an Italian aperitif that's made from bitter orange and rhubarb. It's similar to Campari but lighter, and in the summer, this cocktail of Prosecco, Aperol, and sparkling water is the most refreshing drink.

Ice cubes
1 (750 ml) bottle Prosecco, chilled
12 ounces Aperol, such as Barbieri
San Pellegrino or other sparkling water, chilled
6 half-round slices of orange or blood orange

For each drink, fill a 14- to 16-ounce tumbler three-quarters full with ice. Fill each glass two-thirds full with Prosecco, add 2 ounces of the Aperol, a splash of San Pellegrino, and an orange slice, and stir. Serve ice cold.

perfect potato pancakes

makes 24 to 30 pancakes

I have always made potato pancakes with grated potatoes for crisp pancakes, but I've also thought about making them with mashed potatoes for creamy ones. When I read that Andrew Zimmern's grandmother made potato pancakes with both of them together, I had an aha! moment. Even better!

   1 pound Yukon Gold potatoes, unpeeled and 1-inch-diced
      Kosher salt and freshly ground black pepper
   2 pounds Idaho baking potatoes, peeled
   1 large yellow onion
   2 extra-large eggs, lightly beaten
  ½ cup panko (Japanese bread flakes) or matzo meal
   3 tablespoons minced fresh chives, plus extra for serving
      Unsalted butter
      Good olive oil
      Sour cream, for serving

Place the Yukon Gold potatoes in a large pot of boiling salted water and simmer for 15 to 20 minutes, until very tender when tested with a knife. Drain and pass through a ricer or the coarsest blade of a food mill into a large bowl and set aside.

Grate the Idaho potatoes lengthwise in long shreds, either by hand or in a food processor fitted with the coarsest grating disk. Place the potatoes on a kitchen towel, squeeze out most of the liquid, and transfer to the bowl with the cooked potatoes. (Don't worry—they'll turn pink.) Grate the onion either by hand or in the food processor and stir into the potatoes along with the eggs, panko, chives, 2 teaspoons salt, and 1 teaspoon pepper.

Heat 2 tablespoons of butter with 1 tablespoon of olive oil in a large (12-inch) sauté pan over medium-high heat, until sizzling. Drop heaping tablespoons of the potato mixture into the skillet (you want them to be messy). Flatten the pancakes lightly with a metal spatula and cook for 2 to 3 minutes on each side, until browned. Continue adding butter and oil, as needed, to fry the remaining batter. Serve hot with sour cream and chives.

MAKE AHEAD
Prepare the mixture and refrigerate for several hours. Fry just before serving or up to 30 minutes ahead. Place on a sheet pan, and reheat at 400 degrees for 5 to 10 minutes.

limoncello vodka collins

makes 4 to 6 drinks

My friends Deborah Burke and Peter McCann played around with an old-fashioned Tom Collins recipe and came up with this drink. Freshly squeezed lemon juice is the key—it's basically a tall, cool glass of lemonade with a limoncello and vodka kick! I tested it with sugar on the rim of the glass but it was too sweet, and I tried salt but it was too salty. The two mixed together, though, made this drink even better!

1¼ cups freshly squeezed lemon juice (5 to 7 lemons), divided

2 tablespoons kosher salt

2 tablespoons granulated sugar

1½ cups good vodka, such as Grey Goose

6 tablespoons sugar syrup (see note)

¼ cup Italian limoncello liqueur

1½ cups cold sparkling water, such as San Pellegrino

Ice cubes

Thinly sliced lemon rounds, for serving

To make this sugar syrup, combine 1 cup of sugar with ½ cup water in a small saucepan, bring to a boil, and cook until the sugar dissolves. Cool.

For the salt-sugar rim on the glasses, pour ¼ cup of the lemon juice in a shallow bowl. Combine the salt and sugar on a small plate. Dip the rim of the glasses first in the lemon juice and then dip them lightly in the salt-sugar mixture. Set aside to dry.

Combine the vodka, the 1 cup of lemon juice, sugar syrup, and limoncello in a large pitcher. Just before serving, pour in the sparkling water and stir.

Fill each glass with ice. Pour the cocktail mixture over the ice, garnish each drink with a slice of lemon, and serve ice cold.

MAKE AHEAD
Prep the glasses. Combine the vodka, lemon juice, sugar syrup, and limoncello in a pitcher and refrigerate for up to 4 hours. Stir in the sparkling water just before serving.

smoked salmon pizzas

makes 6 small pizzas; serves 12 for appetizers, 6 for lunch

This pizza is inspired by Wolfgang Puck, the founder and chef of Spago and many other spectacular restaurants around the world. He made a smoked salmon pizza for Joan Collins one night and she insisted on having it whenever she came to dinner. Crisp warm pizza, creamy mascarpone, and smoked salmon on top? If I were Joan Collins, I'd insist on having it, too!

FOR THE DOUGH

1¼ cups warm (100 to 110 degrees) water

2 (¼-ounce) packages active dry yeast

1 tablespoon honey

Good olive oil

4 cups all-purpose flour, divided, plus extra for kneading

Kosher salt and freshly ground black pepper

Fine cornmeal

TO ASSEMBLE

8 ounces Italian mascarpone

1 tablespoon minced fresh chives, plus extra for garnish

½ to ¾ pound thinly sliced smoked salmon, preferably Scottish or Norwegian

Salmon roe, for garnish (optional)

For the dough, combine the water, yeast, honey, and 3 tablespoons of olive oil in the bowl of an electric mixer fitted with the dough hook. Add 3 cups of the flour, then 2 teaspoons of salt and mix for about 10 minutes, slowly adding up to 1 more cup of flour to just keep the dough from sticking to the bowl. When the dough is ready, turn it out onto a floured board and knead by hand a dozen times. It should be smooth and elastic. Brush a medium bowl with olive oil, place the dough in the bowl, and turn it several times to cover lightly with oil. Cover the bowl with a clean, damp kitchen towel and set aside at room temperature for 30 minutes, until doubled in size.

MAKE AHEAD
You can make the dough up to 4 hours in advance and refrigerate until ready to use.

Divide the dough into 6 equal parts and roll each one into a smooth ball. Place the balls on a sheet pan and cover them with the damp towel. Allow the dough to rest for 10 minutes.

Preheat the oven to 500 degrees. Sprinkle 3 sheet pans with cornmeal.

If you've chilled the dough, leave it at room temperature for 30 minutes to allow it to come to room temperature. Press each piece of dough into a circle with your fingertips. Stretch the balls of dough into rough 8-inch circles and place them on the prepared sheet pans.

Brush the dough with olive oil and bake for 12 to 15 minutes, until lightly browned and crisp, rotating the pans to bake evenly. Set aside to cool slightly.

Whisk the mascarpone with 1 tablespoon of the chives, ½ teaspoon salt, and ½ teaspoon pepper. Spread the mixture on the pizzas, place one layer of smoked salmon on top, sprinkle with chives, and add a large mound of salmon roe in the middle, if using. Place the pizzas on a serving board, cut them into wedges, and serve immediately.

fried oysters with lemon saffron aioli

serves 4 to 6

This is a long recipe but you can make it in two parts and it's so worth it! The garlicky aioli with spicy saffron is the perfect partner to the hot, crunchy oysters. I make the aioli ahead and refrigerate it. Before serving, fry the oysters (it takes just a few minutes!) and stir a tablespoon of hot water into the aioli before spooning it onto the oyster shells.

Zest the lemons before you juice them.

FOR THE AIOLI

- 3 tablespoons freshly squeezed lemon juice, at room temperature (see note)
- ½ teaspoon saffron threads
- 2 extra-large egg yolks, at room temperature
- 1 tablespoon minced garlic (3 cloves)
  Kosher salt and freshly ground black pepper
- 1 cup good olive oil
- ½ cup canola oil
- 2 teaspoons grated lemon zest (2 lemons)

FOR THE OYSTERS

- 20 large, freshly shucked oysters, liquor and rounded bottom shells reserved
  Canola oil, for frying (I used 1½ quarts)
- 1 extra-large egg
- ⅓ cup buttermilk, shaken
- ¾ cup all-purpose flour
- ½ cup fine yellow cornmeal, such as Quaker
- ½ cup panko (Japanese bread flakes)
  Pinch of ground cayenne pepper

Preheat the oven to 250 degrees. Line a sheet pan with paper towels.

For the aioli, put the lemon juice and saffron in the bowl of a food processor fitted with the steel blade and allow them to sit for 5 minutes. Add the egg yolks, garlic, 2 teaspoons salt, and 1 teaspoon black pepper and process for 15 seconds. Combine the olive and canola oils in a glass measuring cup. With the

MAKE AHEAD
Prepare the aioli, cover, and refrigerate for up to 5 days.

machine running, very slowly pour the oils through the feed tube, until the mixture is a thick emulsion. Add the lemon zest and 1 teaspoon of water and pulse to combine.

Refrigerate the oysters while heating the oil. Pour 1 inch of canola oil into a medium (10-inch) heavy-bottomed pot or Dutch oven, such as Le Creuset. Heat over medium-high heat until the oil registers 350 degrees on a candy thermometer.

In a small bowl, whisk together the egg, ⅓ cup of the oyster liquor (discard the rest), the buttermilk, and 1 teaspoon salt. In a shallow bowl, combine the flour, cornmeal, panko, 2 teaspoons salt, 1 teaspoon black pepper, and the cayenne pepper.

Place the shells on a serving platter and put a heaping tablespoon of aioli in each.

When the oil is hot, dip each oyster in the egg mixture and then roll it in the flour mixture. Fry the oysters in batches of 6 to 8 for 60 to 90 seconds, turning once, cooking until golden brown. Don't crowd them! Remove with a wire strainer and transfer to the prepared sheet pan. Keep warm in the oven for up to 10 minutes while you fry the remaining oysters.

Place a fried oyster on each prepared shell, sprinkle with salt, and serve hot.

french 75

makes 4 drinks

Dear friends of ours who love great cocktails brought me Brian Van Flandern's inspired first cocktail book, called Vintage Cocktails, *and I've bought every book he's written since. This very special Champagne cocktail from his book is both sweet and lemony, with the rich flavor of Cognac.*

½ cup (4 ounces) VS or VSOP Cognac
½ cup (4 ounces) simple syrup (see note)
⅓ cup (3 ounces) freshly squeezed lemon juice (2 lemons)
2 cups ice cubes
1 (750 ml) bottle good Champagne, chilled
4 long strips of lemon zest (see note)

Pour the Cognac, simple syrup, and lemon juice into a cocktail shaker and add the ice. Shake for at least 30 seconds (it's longer than you think!). Pour the mixture into 4 Champagne flutes to fill each glass about two-thirds full. Fill the glasses with Champagne, garnish with the lemon zest, and serve ice cold.

Use a sharp vegetable peeler to zest the lemon in strips, taking care not to get the bitter white pith.

For this simple syrup, combine 1 cup water and 1 cup sugar in a small saucepan, bring to a boil, and cook until the sugar dissolves. Cool.

asparagus & fennel soup

maple-roasted carrot salad

kale salad with pancetta & pecorino

camembert & prosciutto tartines

tomato carpaccio

arugula with prosciutto & burrata

butternut squash & ricotta bruschettas

artichokes with lemon-tarragon aioli

lentil & kielbasa salad

soups, salads & lunch

asparagus & fennel soup

homemade chicken stock

"16 bean" pasta e fagioli

spicy sweet potato empanadas

zucchini & leek frittata

fiesta corn & avocado salad

anna's tomato tart

tarragon shrimp salad

camping trip

Sometimes it's possible to pinpoint that moment when your thinking about food completely changes, when something as basic as a slice of crusty bread, a piece of runny cheese, or a perfectly ripe peach shows you how delicious the simplest food can be. For me, that moment came in France.

After the army, Jeffrey decided to study foreign policy at the Johns Hopkins School of Advanced International Studies in Washington, D.C. We had four months between his last army post and the beginning of school and nothing at all planned—and, of course, we had almost no money. At that time students could buy a round-trip plane ticket from New York to Brussels on Sabena airline for $99, so we got ourselves two tickets and set off on a magical trip that would dramatically alter both of our lives.

We bought a tent, sleeping bags, and a small camping gas stove because we knew we couldn't possibly afford to stay in hotels and eat in restaurants. Instead, we planned to buy food at local markets and I would cook in our tent.

Our first stop was Paris and it was a revelation to me. I had always thought about French food as "cuisine" with complicated preparations and slowly simmered sauces. Instead, I discovered French street markets and simple, seasonal food that was based on incredibly good ingredients. We bought baskets of Gariguette strawberries that tasted like strawberry preserves, and ripe peaches that would drip down your arm as you ate them. I'd never tasted anything like that! We'd have a rotisserie chicken for dinner, some fresh tomatoes, and runny cheese and we were good to go. In those days you couldn't even buy freshly baked bread in the United States, yet every little town in France had a *boulangerie* with four kinds of baguettes alone! In Paris I remember going crazy at Poilâne bakery on rue Cherche-Midi and the street market on boulevard Raspail. If anyone had told me then that decades later I would live near these two magical places, I would have thought they were insane.

The tartines on page 51, made with Poilâne bread, salty prosciutto, and ripe Camembert are one of my favorite things to order when we visit Poilâne today, and when I make them for us here at home, it reminds us both of that amazing trip, and of how extraordinary simple food can be when it's made with really good ingredients.

Cooking in our tent

maple-roasted carrot salad

serves 4 for lunch, 6 as a side dish

This may be my favorite salad ever. With the sweet caramelized carrots, peppery arugula, creamy goat cheese, and salty Marcona almonds, every bite is so interesting!

2 pounds carrots, preferably with leafy tops
Good olive oil
Kosher salt and freshly ground black pepper
¼ cup pure Grade A maple syrup
⅔ cup dried cranberries
⅔ cup freshly squeezed orange juice (2 oranges)
3 tablespoons sherry wine vinegar
2 garlic cloves, grated on a Microplane
6 ounces baby arugula
6 ounces goat cheese, such as Montrachet, medium-diced
⅔ cup roasted, salted Marcona almonds

Preheat the oven to 425 degrees.

Trim and scrub the carrots. If the carrots are more than 1 inch in diameter, cut them in half lengthwise. Cut the carrots in large diagonal slices 1 inch wide × 2 inches long (they will shrink when they roast) and place in a medium bowl with ¼ cup of olive oil, 1 teaspoon salt, and ½ teaspoon pepper. Toss well and transfer to two sheet pans. (If you use just one, they'll steam instead of roasting.) Roast for 20 minutes, tossing once, until the carrots are tender. Transfer all the carrots to one of the sheet pans, add the maple syrup, toss, and roast for 10 to 15 minutes, until the edges are caramelized. Watch them carefully! Toss with a metal spatula and set aside for 10 minutes.

Meanwhile, combine the cranberries and orange juice in a small saucepan, bring to a simmer, then set aside for 10 minutes.

In a small bowl, combine the vinegar, garlic, and ½ teaspoon salt. Whisk in 3 tablespoons of olive oil. Place the arugula in a large bowl and add the carrots, cranberries (with their liquid), goat cheese, almonds, and the vinaigrette. Toss with large spoons, sprinkle with salt, and serve at room temperature.

MAKE AHEAD
Prep all the ingredients. Cook the cranberries and make the vinaigrette and refrigerate for up to a day. Roast the carrots and assemble the salad just before serving.

kale salad with pancetta & pecorino

serves 4

Okay, I know there is a rebellion against kale going on. I'm not suggesting you eat it every day but it has great flavor and it's also so good for you. This is a simple kale salad with a garlicky Caesar dressing. Warm pancetta, crisp croutons, and spicy Pecorino cheese add lots of flavor and crunch!

    4 anchovy fillets, drained
    1 large garlic clove
    1 tablespoon Dijon mustard
    2 extra-large egg yolks, at room temperature
    ⅓ cup freshly squeezed lemon juice, at room temperature
      (2 lemons)
      Kosher salt and freshly ground black pepper
    ⅔ cup good olive oil, plus extra to cook the pancetta
    ¼ cup freshly grated Italian Pecorino cheese
    1 pound lacinato kale (also called dinosaur or
      Tuscan kale)
    4 ounces pancetta, small-diced
    1 cup (½-inch-diced) bread cubes, crusts removed
    ½ cup shaved Italian Pecorino cheese (2 ounces)

For the dressing, place the anchovies, garlic, mustard, egg yolks, lemon juice, 1 teaspoon salt, and ½ teaspoon pepper in the bowl of a food processor fitted with the steel blade. Process for 30 seconds, until smooth. With the processor running, slowly pour the olive oil through the feed tube, until the mixture emulsifies. Add the grated Pecorino and process just until combined. Transfer to a container and refrigerate until ready to use.

Wash the kale and spin it dry in a salad spinner. Remove the rib from each leaf. Stack the leaves and slice them thinly crosswise, as you would cole slaw. Place the kale in a large bowl and toss with enough dressing to moisten.

Heat 1 tablespoon of olive oil in a medium (10-inch) sauté pan. Add the pancetta and cook over medium heat for 6 to 8 minutes, tossing frequently, until browned and crisp. Transfer the

MAKE AHEAD
Prepare the dressing, slice the kale, and store separately in the fridge. Just before serving, cook the pancetta and toasted bread cubes, toss the kale with the dressing, and complete the recipe.

pancetta with a slotted spoon to a plate lined with paper towels. Add the bread cubes to the pan, sprinkle with salt, and sauté for 5 to 7 minutes, tossing frequently, until evenly browned. Add the pancetta, toasted bread, and shaved Pecorino to the kale and toss with large spoons. Serve at room temperature.

tomato carpaccio

serves 4

Carpaccio is a classic Italian dish made with thin slices of raw beef drizzled with olive oil and lemon juice and often garnished with capers and Parmesan cheese. I thought it would be fun to do a variation using red summer tomatoes that resemble the beef and a Caesar dressing to drizzle on top with the capers and Parmesan.

2 extra-large egg yolks, at room temperature

2 teaspoons Dijon mustard, at room temperature

1 tablespoon chopped garlic (3 cloves)

2 anchovy fillets, drained

½ cup freshly squeezed lemon juice, at room temperature (2 to 3 lemons)

Kosher salt and freshly ground black pepper

¾ cup good olive oil

¼ cup canola oil

½ cup freshly grated Italian Parmesan cheese

4 to 5 large, firm, ripe red summer tomatoes, preferably heirloom

½ teaspoon fleur de sel

2 tablespoons capers, drained

¼ cup julienned fresh basil leaves

2-ounce chunk of Italian Parmesan cheese, shaved with a vegetable peeler

Place the egg yolks, mustard, garlic, anchovies, lemon juice, 2½ teaspoons kosher salt, and 1 teaspoon pepper in a food processor fitted with the steel blade and process for 15 seconds. Combine the olive and canola oils in a glass measuring cup. With the food processor running, slowly pour the oils in a thin stream down the feed tube, as you would to make mayonnaise. Add the grated Parmesan and pulse to combine. The mixture will be thin enough to drizzle on the tomatoes.

Pour a puddle of dressing in the middle of 4 dinner plates. Core the tomatoes and slice crosswise with a serrated knife about ⅜ inch thick. Arrange overlapping slices of tomatoes

MAKE AHEAD
Prepare the dressing ahead and refrigerate. Slice the tomatoes and assemble just before serving.

decoratively on the plates. Sprinkle with the fleur de sel and drizzle more dressing onto the tomatoes with a tablespoon. Sprinkle with the capers, basil, shaved Parmesan, and pepper. Serve at room temperature with a pitcher of extra dressing on the side.

butternut squash & ricotta bruschettas

serves 6

I love the way recipes evolve; I believe this one started with Jean-Georges Vongerichten and I also saw a version from Mark Bittman. Not only do I like the savory-sweet thing of butternut squash and maple syrup, but I also love the creamy ricotta on the crisp toast.

  1 pound butternut squash, peeled and ½- to ¾-inch-diced
    Good olive oil
    Kosher salt and freshly ground black pepper
  ⅛ teaspoon crushed red pepper flakes
  2 tablespoons unsalted butter
  3 cups sliced yellow onions (2 onions)
  2 tablespoons apple cider vinegar
  2 tablespoons pure Grade A maple syrup
    Apple cider or apple juice (optional)
  6 (½-inch-thick) slices rustic country bread, toasted (see note)
1½ cups fresh ricotta, homemade (recipe follows) or store-bought

Preheat the oven to 425 degrees.

Place the squash, 2½ tablespoons olive oil, 1 teaspoon salt, ½ teaspoon black pepper, and the red pepper flakes on a sheet pan, toss, and spread out in one layer. Roast for 25 to 35 minutes, until very tender and starting to brown on the edges, tossing once with a metal spatula during roasting. Set aside.

Meanwhile, heat the butter and 2 tablespoons olive oil in a medium (10-inch) sauté pan. Add the onions and cook over medium to medium-low heat for 12 to 15 minutes, tossing occasionally, until golden brown. Add the vinegar and maple syrup and simmer over medium heat for 4 to 6 minutes, until the liquid is reduced. When the squash is tender, add it to the sauté pan with the onions and mash it lightly with a dinner fork.

(recipe continues)

To toast the bread, brush with olive oil, sprinkle with salt and pepper, and toast in a 350-degree oven for 12 to 15 minutes.

MAKE AHEAD
Prepare the butternut squash mixture and refrigerate for up to 2 days. Reheat adding a few tablespoons of apple cider. Assemble the bruschettas just before serving.

If the mixture is a little dry, add a few tablespoons of apple cider to moisten. Taste for seasonings and reheat over low heat, if necessary.

To assemble the bruschettas, spread a thick layer of ricotta on each toast and spoon the squash mixture on top. Sprinkle with salt and serve warm.

homemade ricotta

makes about 2 cups

4 cups whole milk

2 cups heavy cream

1 teaspoon kosher salt

3 tablespoons good white wine vinegar

Set a fine-mesh sieve over a deep bowl. Dampen 2 layers of cheesecloth with water and line the sieve with the cheesecloth.

Pour the milk and cream into a stainless-steel saucepan. Stir in the salt and bring to a rolling boil over medium heat, stirring occasionally. Turn off the heat and stir in the vinegar. Allow the mixture to stand for one minute until it curdles. It will separate into a thick part (the curds) and a milky part (the whey).

Pour the mixture into the cheesecloth-lined sieve and allow it to drain at room temperature for 20 to 25 minutes, occasionally discarding the liquid that accumulates in the bowl. The longer you let the mixture drain, the thicker the ricotta will be. Transfer the ricotta to a bowl, discarding the cheesecloth and any remaining whey. Use immediately or cover with plastic wrap and refrigerate. The ricotta will keep refrigerated for 4 to 5 days.

garlic toasts

makes 12 toasts

This is a great way to use up leftover baguettes. The toasts are wonderful to serve with a salad but also on top of soup or with dips and cheeses.

½ **French baguette**
2 **to 3 tablespoons good olive oil**
  Kosher salt and freshly ground black pepper
1 **garlic clove, halved lengthwise**

Preheat the oven to 400 degrees.

Slice the baguette ¼ inch thick in 12 long diagonal slices.

Lay the slices in one layer on a sheet pan, brush each with olive oil, and sprinkle liberally with salt and pepper. Bake the toasts for 15 to 20 minutes, until they are browned and crisp. As soon as they are cool enough to handle, rub one side of each toast with the cut side of the garlic. Serve at room temperature.

MAKE AHEAD
Prepare the toasts a day or two in advance and cool. Store in a plastic bag at room temperature.

artichokes with lemon-tarragon aioli

serves 5 to 6

Aioli is a classic Provençal garlic mayonnaise that is traditionally served with bouillabaisse, simple meats, grilled fish, and vegetables. I've made this aioli with garlic, fresh tarragon (which has a slight anise flavor), and lots of freshly squeezed lemon juice to brighten the earthy flavor of the artichokes.

> 5 large or 6 medium artichokes
> 1 lemon, halved
> 1 cup white wine
> 2 tablespoons good olive oil
> 2 tablespoons Pernod liqueur
> 1 large garlic clove, thinly sliced
>   Lemon-Tarragon Aioli (recipe follows)

Trim the artichoke stems so they sit upright on a cutting board. Remove and discard the top inch of each artichoke with a large knife and trim off the top of each spiny leaf with scissors. As you cut each artichoke, rub the cut edges with half a lemon to keep them from browning. Place the artichokes stem end down in a stockpot that's large enough to hold them side by side without crowding. Add the wine, olive oil, Pernod, garlic, and enough water so the artichokes are floating (you may need to add more hot water as they cook). Thinly slice the remaining half a lemon and add it to the pot. Bring to a boil, lower the heat, cover, and simmer for 45 minutes to 1 hour, until the artichokes are tender when pierced through the base with a sharp knife. Remove the artichokes, drain, and allow to sit at room temperature until ready to serve.

Serve one artichoke per person warm, at room temperature, or chilled, with the lemon-tarragon aioli on the side for dipping. If the aioli is too thick, you can whisk in a tablespoon of warm water to thin it.

MAKE AHEAD
Prepare the artichokes and aioli and refrigerate for up to 3 days.

lentil & kielbasa salad

serves 6

I worked on lentil salad for years and couldn't get the flavor right. One day, I was having lunch with a friend in Paris and I asked her what the secret was and she said that they put a turnip in the cooking liquid—and then throw away the turnip! Thick slices of kielbasa and goat cheese toasts make this a hearty winter lunch.

Good olive oil

2 cups medium-diced leeks, white and light green parts

1 cup (¼-inch-diced) carrots (2 carrots)

1 pound green French Le Puy lentils, rinsed and drained

1 whole peeled onion stuck with 6 whole dried cloves

1 small turnip

1 tablespoon minced garlic (3 cloves)

3 tablespoons Dijon mustard

5 tablespoons good red wine vinegar

Kosher salt and freshly ground black pepper

6 scallions, white and green parts, thinly sliced crosswise

1½ teaspoons chopped fresh thyme leaves

½ cup minced fresh parsley leaves

10 ounces kielbasa, halved lengthwise and sliced ½ inch thick diagonally

6 (½-inch-thick) diagonal slices of a baguette

4 ounces creamy herbed goat cheese, such as Montrachet

Heat 2 tablespoons of olive oil in a large saucepan, add the leeks, and cook uncovered over medium heat for 5 minutes. Add the carrots and cook for one minute. Add the lentils, onion, turnip, and 6 cups of water. Bring to a boil, lower the heat, and simmer uncovered for 20 to 25 minutes, until the lentils are tender. Discard the onion and turnip and drain the lentils, reserving some of the cooking liquid. Place the lentils in a large bowl.

Meanwhile, in a small bowl or glass measuring cup, whisk together the garlic, mustard, vinegar, 2 teaspoons salt, and 1 teaspoon pepper. Slowly whisk in ½ cup olive oil, add to the lentils, and toss. If it's dry, add a few tablespoons of the reserved cooking liquid.

MAKE AHEAD
Prepare the salad, cover, and refrigerate for up to 3 days, saving some of the cooking liquid to add later. Prepare the goat cheese toasts just before serving.

Add the scallions, thyme, parsley, kielbasa, 2 teaspoons salt, and 1 teaspoon pepper and toss. Set aside to cool.

Toast the baguette slices and spread with the goat cheese. Taste the salad for seasonings and serve at room temperature with the goat cheese toasts.

asparagus & fennel soup

serves 6 to 8

When asparagus is plentiful, I make lots of this soup and freeze it for a quick lunch. Most rich soups are thickened with potatoes or heavy cream; instead, this soup gets its texture from rice, which makes it surprisingly silky smooth. Asparagus and fennel are great together because each one makes the other taste better. The hit of Pernod and basil makes the soup even more delicious.

2½ tablespoons good olive oil

2½ tablespoons unsalted butter

5 cups (¾-inch-diced) fennel, tops and cores removed (2 fennel bulbs)

3 cups chopped leeks, white and light green parts (2 leeks) (see note)

2½ cups chopped yellow onions (2 onions)

1 pound medium-thick asparagus

½ cup long-grain white rice

8 cups good chicken stock, preferably homemade (recipe follows)

3 large sprigs fresh thyme, tied with kitchen string

Kosher salt and freshly ground black pepper

½ cup julienned fresh basil leaves, plus extra for garnish

2 tablespoons Pernod liqueur

½ cup half-and-half

Freshly grated Italian Parmesan cheese, for serving

In a large (11-inch) pot or Dutch oven such as Le Creuset, heat the olive oil and butter over medium heat and add the fennel, leeks, and onions. Cut or break off the tough bottoms of the asparagus and discard. Cut off 8 (2-inch) tips from the asparagus and reserve. Slice the remaining stalks ½ inch thick crosswise and add them to the pot. Cook the vegetables for 20 minutes, stirring occasionally, until very tender.

Add the rice to the vegetables, pour in the chicken stock, add the thyme, 2 teaspoons salt, and 1 teaspoon pepper, and bring to a boil. Lower the heat and simmer for 30 minutes, stirring

Be sure to wash the leeks thoroughly; they can be very sandy.

occasionally, until the rice is very tender. Off the heat, stir in the basil and Pernod. Discard the thyme bundle.

Meanwhile, bring a small saucepan of water to a boil. Add the reserved asparagus tips, cook for 2 minutes, drain, and transfer to a bowl of ice water. Set aside.

Puree the soup with an immersion blender. (You can use a regular blender but be careful not to overfill it!) Stir in the half-and-half, taste for seasonings, and reheat over low heat. Ladle into soup bowls and garnish with julienned basil, Parmesan cheese, and a blanched asparagus tip.

Store asparagus in the refrigerator like flowers; cut the ends and stand upright in a beaker of water.

MAKE AHEAD
Prepare the soup completely and refrigerate for up to 5 days or freeze for up to 6 months.

homemade chicken stock

makes 6 quarts

I have to include this recipe in every book because it's the basis for so many of my dishes. Of course, you can use canned stock or broth but this is easy to make and the difference it makes in the finished dish is astonishing. When I'm at home, I throw everything into a big pot and let it simmer away. Four hours later, I have quarts of chicken stock to store in the freezer and the house smells wonderful.

3 (5-pound) roasting chickens
3 large yellow onions, unpeeled and quartered
6 carrots, unpeeled and halved crosswise
4 stalks celery with leaves, cut into thirds crosswise
4 parsnips unpeeled and halved crosswise
20 sprigs flat-leaf parsley
15 sprigs fresh thyme
20 sprigs fresh dill
1 head garlic, unpeeled and cut in half crosswise
2 tablespoons kosher salt
2 teaspoons whole black peppercorns (not ground)

MAKE AHEAD
Pack the stock in containers and refrigerate for up to 5 days or freeze for up to 4 months.

Place the chickens, onions, carrots, celery, parsnips, parsley, thyme, dill, garlic, salt, and peppercorns in a 16- to 20-quart stockpot. Add 7 quarts of water and bring to a boil. Lower the heat and simmer uncovered for 4 hours, skimming off any foam that comes to the top. Set aside until cool enough to handle. Strain the entire contents of the pot through a sieve or colander and discard the solids.

"16 bean" pasta e fagioli

serves 6

Pasta e fagioli is a classic Italian soup with pasta and white beans. I'm always looking for new ways to make old-fashioned dishes and Goya's 16-bean soup mix was the perfect change. This is thick enough to be a hearty meal on a cold winter day. I added a splash of red wine vinegar at the end, which really wakes up the flavor of the soup.

1 (1-pound) bag Goya 16 Bean Soup Mix

2 tablespoons good olive oil, plus extra for serving

6 ounces pancetta, ¼-inch-diced

1 large onion, chopped

1 tablespoon minced garlic (3 cloves)

½ teaspoon crushed red pepper flakes

1 (28-ounce) can crushed tomatoes, preferably San Marzano

1 cup dry red wine

4 to 6 cups good chicken stock, preferably homemade (page 68)

Kosher salt and freshly ground black pepper

1 cup miniature pasta, such as ditalini or tubettini

½ cup freshly grated Italian Parmesan cheese, plus extra for serving

1 tablespoon good red wine vinegar

Julienned fresh basil leaves, for serving

The day before you plan to make the soup, place the bean mix in a large bowl, add cold water to cover by 2 inches, and refrigerate overnight. The next day, drain the beans, rinse under cold running water, and drain again. Place the beans in a large pot with 8 cups of cold water. Bring to a boil, lower the heat, and simmer for 1 hour. Stir occasionally and skim off any foam that rises to the top. The beans should be very tender and the skin will peel away when you blow on a bean.

Meanwhile, heat the oil in a medium (10-inch) stockpot or Dutch oven over medium heat. Add the pancetta and onion and sauté over medium to medium-high heat for 12 to 18 minutes, until browned. Add the garlic and red pepper flakes and sauté

MAKE AHEAD
Prepare the soup and refrigerate for up to 5 days or freeze for up to 6 months. Add more chicken stock or water if the soup is too thick.

for one minute. Add the tomatoes, wine, 4 cups of the chicken stock, 1 tablespoon salt, and 1 teaspoon black pepper and turn off the heat.

Drain the beans and add two-thirds of them to the soup. Pass the remaining beans through a food mill, discarding the skins. Stir the bean puree and the pasta into the soup, bring to a boil, lower the heat, and simmer for 20 to 30 minutes, stirring occasionally, until the pasta is tender. Add up to 2 more cups chicken stock if the soup is too thick. Stir in the Parmesan and the vinegar. Ladle the soup into large shallow bowls and add a swirl of olive oil, a sprinkle of Parmesan, and some basil. Serve hot with extra Parmesan on the side.

spicy sweet potato empanadas

makes 8 empanadas

While I was in San Francisco filming my TV show, we came across a bevy of fantastic food trucks. One truck made empanadas filled with all kinds of international flavors, which inspired me to come home and make these sweet potato empanadas seasoned with orange, maple syrup, and chipotle chile powder. Baking them in puff pastry instead of frying them in empanada dough makes these so much lighter!

1 pound sweet potatoes, scrubbed (2 potatoes)
  Good olive oil
¼ cup sour cream
1½ tablespoons unsalted butter, diced
1½ tablespoons pure Grade A maple syrup
½ teaspoon chipotle chile powder
½ teaspoon grated orange zest
2 tablespoons freshly squeezed orange juice
  Kosher salt and freshly ground black pepper
2 sheets (1 box) frozen puff pastry, such as Pepperidge Farm, defrosted in the refrigerator
1 egg beaten with 1 tablespoon of water, for egg wash
  Flaked sea salt, such as Maldon

Preheat the oven to 425 degrees. Line one sheet pan with aluminum foil and another with parchment paper.

Rub the sweet potatoes with olive oil and prick them all over with the tines of a fork. Place the potatoes on the foil-lined sheet pan. Bake for about 1 hour, until very tender when pierced with a knife. Lower the oven to 375 degrees.

Allow the potatoes to cool enough to handle, then peel and discard the skins, placing the potatoes in the bowl of an electric mixer fitted with the paddle attachment. Add the sour cream, butter, maple syrup, chile powder, orange zest, orange juice, 1½ teaspoons kosher salt, and ¾ teaspoon black pepper and mix well. Set aside.

Unfold one sheet of the cold puff pastry on a floured cutting board. Roll the sheet into a 12-inch square with a rolling pin. With a sharp paring knife, cut four 5-inch circles from the

MAKE AHEAD
Prepare the filling up to 2 days ahead. Assemble the empanadas and refrigerate for up to 4 hours. Bake just before serving.

pastry, using a dish as a guide and discarding the scraps. Place a heaping soupspoon of filling on each circle, leaving a 1-inch border. Brush the edges of the circles with the egg wash and fold over, making half circles. Crimp the edges together with the tines of a fork. Repeat with the second sheet of puff pastry. Place on the parchment-lined sheet pan. Chill for 15 minutes.

Brush with the egg wash and sprinkle with the sea salt and pepper. Make 2 small slits in each empanada to allow steam to escape. Bake for 25 to 30 minutes, until puffed and browned. Serve hot.

zucchini & leek frittata

serves 4 to 5

*My friend Devon Fredericks made a zucchini frittata and used the
zucchini flowers to decorate the top. I love when the garnish tells
you exactly what's in the dish and this was a very simple, elegant
presentation. Don't worry; if you can't find zucchini flowers, the frittata is
just as delicious without them.*

- 2 tablespoons good olive oil
- 3 ounces pancetta, ½-inch-diced (see note)
- 2 cups medium-diced leeks, white and light green parts
  (2 leeks)
- 8 to 10 ounces small zucchini, thinly sliced in rounds
- 1 teaspoon fresh thyme leaves, minced
- 8 extra-large eggs
- ½ cup half-and-half
  Kosher salt and freshly ground black pepper
- 5 ounces grated Gruyère cheese, divided
- 3 tablespoons julienned fresh basil leaves
- 5 zucchini flowers (optional)

Preheat the oven to 350 degrees.

Heat the olive oil in a 10-inch ovenproof sauté pan (see note)
over medium heat. Add the pancetta and sauté for 5 minutes,
until it begins to brown. Rinse the leeks well, spin-dry in a salad
spinner, add to the pan, and sauté for another 5 minutes, until
tender. Add the zucchini and thyme and toss. Cook for 5 to
6 minutes, stirring occasionally, until the zucchini is tender.

Meanwhile, in a large bowl, whisk together the eggs, half-and-
half, 1 teaspoon salt, and ½ teaspoon pepper. Stir in two-thirds of
the Gruyère and all of the basil.

Pour the egg mixture into the pan, smoothing the top. Cook
over medium heat for 4 minutes, until the eggs start to set on
the bottom. Sprinkle the top with the remaining Gruyère and
decorate with the zucchini flowers, if using. Transfer the pan to
the oven and bake for 20 to 25 minutes, until puffed and just set
in the center. Allow to sit at room temperature for 5 minutes. Cut
into wedges, sprinkle with salt, and serve hot or warm.

*Have the pancetta
cut in a ½-inch-thick
slice so you can cut
½-inch dice.*

*Use a sauté pan with
sloping sides. It's
sometimes called an
omelet pan.*

MAKE AHEAD
*Prepare the frittata
a few hours ahead
and leave at room
temperature. Reheat
at 350 degrees for
10 to 15 minutes.*

fiesta corn & avocado salad

serves 6

This is a great summer salad: I can get most of the ingredients at my favorite farm stand in Sagaponack plus a few ripe avocados from the grocery store. I made this vinaigrette with olive oil, lime juice, lime zest, and chipotle powder, which really spices it up. This is a perfect side dish for a salad buffet or to serve with grilled chicken.

3 ears corn, preferably yellow, shucked
   Kosher salt and freshly ground black pepper
1 pint heirloom cherry tomatoes, halved through the stem
1 Holland orange bell pepper, cored, seeded, and ½-inch-diced
½ cup medium-diced red onion
2 jalapeño peppers, seeds and ribs removed, minced
1½ teaspoons grated lime zest
¼ cup freshly squeezed lime juice (3 limes)
2 tablespoons good olive oil
1 teaspoon minced garlic
¼ teaspoon chipotle chile powder
2 ripe Hass avocados, large-diced
   Juice of 1 lemon

To cut the corn, shuck it, cut the stem end flat, stand it upright, and cut close to the cob. (I cut the corn onto a paper towel so I can pick up the towel and transfer the corn to the bowl.)

Cook the corn in a large pot of boiling salted water for 5 to 7 minutes, until just tender. Cool for 5 minutes and cut the kernels off the cob, cutting close to the cob with a sharp knife. Place the kernels in a large bowl with the tomatoes, bell pepper, onion, and jalapeño peppers.

In a small bowl or glass measuring cup, whisk together the lime zest, lime juice, olive oil, garlic, chile powder, 1 teaspoon salt, and ½ teaspoon black pepper. Pour the dressing over the vegetables and toss.

In a separate bowl, gently toss the avocados and lemon juice together, making sure the avocado is coated in lemon juice. Add to the vegetables, sprinkle with 1 teaspoon salt and ½ teaspoon black pepper, and carefully fold together without breaking up the avocados. Sprinkle with salt and serve cold or at room temperature.

MAKE AHEAD
Prepare the salad, except the avocados, and refrigerate. Just before serving, add the avocados and serve at room temperature.

anna's tomato tart

serves 6

This recipe is inspired by my dear late friend Anna Pump. She sold so many of these tarts over the thirty-five years that she owned and ran Loaves & Fishes that the cooks would complain that they couldn't make one more tart. It's a perfect summer lunch with a green salad.

FOR THE CRUST

- 2½ cups all-purpose flour
- Kosher salt
- 12 tablespoons (1½ sticks) cold unsalted butter, ½-inch-diced
- 2 cold extra-large egg yolks
- ½ cup ice water
- 2½ pounds dried beans, for baking the crust (optional)

FOR THE FILLING

- 2½ pounds firm medium (2½-inch) tomatoes, cored and sliced ¼ inch thick (see note)
- 1 cup whole fresh parsley leaves, lightly packed
- ½ cup coarsely chopped fresh basil leaves, lightly packed (see note)
- 3 large garlic cloves
- 1 tablespoon fresh thyme leaves
- Kosher salt and freshly ground black pepper
- ½ cup good olive oil
- 6 tablespoons Dijon mustard
- ¾ pound grated Gruyère cheese (1 pound with rind)
- ½ cup plus 2 tablespoons freshly grated Italian Parmesan cheese

I use the firm, small red tomatoes on the vine.

Wash the basil leaves and dry them on kitchen towels before measuring.

Place the flour and 1 teaspoon of salt in the bowl of a food processor fitted with the steel blade. Add the butter and pulse 12 to 15 times, until the butter is the size of peas. Add the egg yolks and pulse a few times to combine. With the motor running, add the ice water through the feed tube and pulse until

(recipe continues)

the dough starts to come together. Dump onto a floured board and roll it into a flat disk. Wrap in plastic wrap and refrigerate for 30 minutes.

Preheat the oven to 400 degrees. Line a sheet pan with parchment paper.

Meanwhile, place the tomatoes in a large bowl. Put the parsley, basil, garlic, thyme, 1 teaspoon salt, and 1 teaspoon pepper in the bowl of a food processor fitted with the steel blade and process until finely minced. With the processor running, pour the olive oil down the feed tube and process until combined. Pour the mixture over the tomatoes and toss gently. Set aside.

Be sure both sheet pans have flat bottoms.

On a well-floured board, roll the dough out to an 11 × 17-inch rectangle and transfer it to the prepared sheet pan. Don't worry if it doesn't fit exactly; you want it to cover most of the bottom of the pan but it can be a little rough on the sides. Place a second sheet pan directly on the pastry (see note) and bake for 15 minutes. (You can also line the pastry with foil and fill it with dried beans.) Remove the top sheet pan (or the beans and foil). Using a dinner fork, pierce the pastry in many places. Bake for another 8 to 10 minutes, until lightly browned. Check the pastry during baking; pierce any spots that bubble up. Allow the crust to cool for 15 minutes.

Lower the oven to 375 degrees. Brush the mustard on the crust with a pastry brush. Sprinkle a thick even layer of Gruyère on the pastry, reserving ½ cup for the top, and sprinkle with the ½ cup of Parmesan. Place overlapping tomatoes in rows on top. If there is a little garlic and herb mixture in the bowl, sprinkle it over the tomatoes, but if there is liquid in the bowl, strain it through a very-fine-mesh strainer, discard the liquid, and sprinkle the garlic and herb mixture on the tomatoes. Sprinkle the reserved ½ cup of Gruyère and the remaining 2 tablespoons of Parmesan on top. Bake for 30 minutes.

Cool slightly, cut into squares, and serve warm or at room temperature.

tarragon shrimp salad

serves 6

My dear friend Johanne Killeen owns Al Forno restaurant in Providence, Rhode Island, one of my favorite restaurants in the world. Johanne taught me to cook shrimp by putting them in cold water and slowly raising the heat. These are the tenderest, most flavorful shrimp I've ever had and they make a great salad with scallions and tarragon.

2 pounds (16- to 20-count) peeled and deveined shrimp (2½ pounds in the shell)

3 tablespoons Pernod liqueur

Kosher salt and freshly ground black pepper

2 tablespoons freshly squeezed lemon juice

1 cup small-diced celery

¾ cup thinly sliced scallions, white and green parts (4 scallions)

2 tablespoons minced fresh tarragon leaves, plus extra for garnish

⅔ cup good mayonnaise, such as Hellmann's

Place the shrimp in a large (8-inch-diameter × 5-inch-high) saucepan and add 8 cups of cold water, the Pernod, and 1 tablespoon salt. Turn the heat to medium high and cook the shrimp uncovered, stirring occasionally, for 8 to 10 minutes, until just firm and pink. Drain in a colander.

Place half the shrimp in a large bowl. Cut the rest of the shrimp sideways through the back with a sharp paring knife and add them to the bowl as well. Allow to cool for 15 minutes. Stir in the lemon juice, 2 teaspoons salt, and 1 teaspoon pepper. Add the celery, scallions, tarragon, and mayonnaise, and combine. Cover and refrigerate for at least 2 hours for the flavors to meld.

Transfer the salad to a serving bowl, sprinkle with extra tarragon and salt, and taste for seasonings. Serve cold or at room temperature.

MAKE AHEAD
Prepare the salad and refrigerate for up to a day. Taste for seasonings just before serving.

filet mignon
with mustard & mushrooms

skillet-roasted lemon chicken

roast chicken with radishes

brisket with onions & leeks

lamb stew with spring vegetables

roasted vegetable paella

dinner

filet mignon with mustard
& mushrooms

cider-roasted pork tenderloins with
roasted plum chutney

moroccan grilled lamb chops

roasted italian meatballs

orecchiette with farm stand
pasta sauce

rigatoni with sausage & fennel

perfect poached lobster & corn
with tarragon butter

roasted salmon tacos

fish & lobster cakes

shrimp & swordfish curry

crusty baked shells & cauliflower

roasted ratatouille with polenta

Summer Filet of Beef
with Béarnaise Mayonnaise
Make It Ahead

inspiration

After our European camping trip Jeffrey and I set up house in Washington, D.C. I went out and bought both volumes of Julia Child's *Mastering the Art of French Cooking,* and I spent the next four years teaching myself how to cook. I had a serious job working in the White House, writing nuclear energy policy papers, but for me the fun started when I came home at night and tried another one of Julia's recipes. On weekends I invited our friends for dinner parties and made traditional French dishes such as lamb stew, tomatoes stuffed with duxelles, ratatouille, coquilles St. Jacques, and clafouti.

At that time a friend of Jeffrey's who worked at the International Monetary Fund invited us to dinner. We liked our friend Dick Erb a lot but he was a guy and I was quite skeptical about his cooking skills. Really? He's making dinner?? I even suggested to Jeffrey that we might have a quick snack before we went to his house.

We arrived at his beautiful townhouse in Alexandria, Virginia (that should have been a clue!), to the smell of freshly baked bread. Dinner that night turned out to be one of the most elegant meals that I'd ever had, with a whole roasted filet of beef, beautifully seasoned and cooked to perfection. (It's still one of Jeffrey's all-time favorites.) The potatoes and vegetables were simply prepared and roasted, and yes, he made his own baguettes from scratch. I was absolutely stunned and what surprised me most is how simple it all was. I remember thinking that this dinner was going to change my cooking forever.

Until that time I'd been challenging myself to make more and more elaborate meals, but that dinner showed me how sophisticated a perfectly prepared dish can be. This became the cornerstone of my cooking philosophy. It's impossible to improve on something as classic as roast chicken. Roast Chicken with Radishes (page 93) is basically two essential ingredients—chicken and radishes—but each ingredient makes the other one taste better, which is what I always look for. The same is true about Port Wine Prunes with Stilton and Walnuts (page 180). Five simple ingredients put together and they are sublime.

We've lost track of our friend now, but I hope he knows how grateful I am for that completely inspiring dinner he made for us more than forty years ago.

skillet-roasted lemon chicken

serves 3

I can't tell you how many times I've made this! I have the butcher butterfly the chicken so all I do is grind the thyme, fennel seeds, salt, and pepper, mix it with olive oil, and brush it on the chicken. When the lemon slices are roasted and caramelized, you can eat them with the chicken.

 2 teaspoons fresh thyme leaves
 1 teaspoon whole fennel seeds
   Kosher salt and freshly ground black pepper
⅓ cup good olive oil
 1 lemon, halved and sliced ¼ inch thick (see note)
 1 yellow onion, halved and sliced ¼ inch thick
 2 large garlic cloves, thinly sliced
 1 (4-pound) chicken, backbone removed and butterflied
½ cup dry white wine, such as Pinot Grigio
   Juice of 1 lemon

Remove the ends of the lemon, cut in half through the stem ends, and slice thinly crosswise.

Preheat the oven to 450 degrees.

Place the thyme, fennel seeds, 1 tablespoon salt, and 1 teaspoon pepper in a mini food processor and process until ground. Pour the olive oil into a small glass measuring cup, stir in the herb mixture, and set aside.

Distribute the lemon slices in a 12-inch cast-iron skillet and distribute the onion and garlic on top. Place the chicken, skin side down, on top of the onion and brush with about half the oil and herb mixture. Turn the chicken skin side up, pat it dry with paper towels (very important!), and brush it all over with the rest of the oil and herb mixture.

Sometimes I sprinkle the chicken with minced fresh rosemary before allowing it to rest.

Roast the chicken for 30 minutes. Pour the wine into the pan (not on the chicken!) and roast for another 10 to 15 minutes, until a meat thermometer inserted into the thickest part of the breast registers 155 to 160 degrees.

Remove the chicken from the oven, sprinkle it with the lemon juice, cover the skillet tightly with aluminum foil, and allow to rest for 10 to 15 minutes. Cut the chicken into quarters or eighths, sprinkle with salt, and serve hot with the pan juices, cooked lemon, and onion.

MAKE AHEAD Assemble the chicken in the pan and refrigerate for a few hours before roasting.

roast chicken with radishes

serves 3

A very chic Frenchwoman made this dish for Jeffrey and me years ago and I've never forgotten it. It seemed so Parisian and elegant and yet it's so simple and earthy. It's basically a chicken roasted with radishes that you can find in any grocery store. If you have heirloom radishes at your local farmers' market, it will be even better!

1 (4- to 4½-pound) roasting chicken, such as Bell & Evans
   Kosher salt and freshly ground black pepper
1 lemon, quartered
6 sprigs fresh thyme
1½ pounds radishes, preferably mixed heirloom, trimmed
   and scrubbed
3 tablespoons unsalted butter, melted

Preheat the oven to 425 degrees.

Place the chicken, breast side up, in a roasting pan or ceramic baking dish just large enough to hold the chicken and radishes, and sprinkle the cavity liberally with salt and pepper. Put the lemon and thyme in the cavity. Tie the legs together with kitchen string and tuck the wings under the body. Cut any larger radishes in half so they are all about the same size and place around the chicken.

Pat the chicken dry with paper towels. Brush the chicken and radishes all over with the melted butter and sprinkle them both liberally with salt and pepper.

Roast for 1 hour and 15 minutes, until the juices run clear when you cut between the leg and thigh. Cover the pan or baking dish with aluminum foil and allow to sit at room temperature for 15 minutes. Carve the chicken and serve with the radishes and pan juices.

MAKE AHEAD
Assemble the entire dish, cover, and refrigerate for up to a day. Brush with butter and roast before serving.

brisket with onions & leeks

serves 8

This amazing dish is based on the most Googled brisket recipe ever! The original came from Nach Waxman, who for many years owned New York's Kitchen Arts & Letters, an iconic store specializing in cookbooks. This is my version of his spectacular (and really easy!) recipe.

1 (5½- to 6-pound) brisket, trimmed with a thin layer of fat
Kosher salt and freshly ground black pepper
3 tablespoons canola oil
¼ cup Wondra flour
1 pound yellow onions, halved and sliced ⅓ inch thick
1 pound red onions, halved and sliced ⅓ inch thick
3 large leeks, white and light green parts only, halved and sliced
6 large garlic cloves, sliced
¾ cup dry red wine
½ cup canned beef stock, such as College Inn
6 sprigs fresh thyme, tied with kitchen string
3 tablespoons tomato paste

Sprinkle the brisket with 2 teaspoons salt, wrap it well, and refrigerate it overnight. This is more important than you think!

The next day, preheat the oven to 350 degrees.

In a very large (13-inch) Dutch oven, such as Le Creuset, heat the oil over medium-high heat. The pot should be large enough for the brisket to lie flat. Sprinkle 1 tablespoon salt and 1 teaspoon pepper all over the brisket. Sprinkle the Wondra flour all over and dust off the excess. Brown the brisket in the oil for 5 minutes on each side, adding more oil if necessary. Transfer to a large (18 × 14 × 2-inch) roasting pan and set aside.

Put the yellow onions, red onions, and leeks in the Dutch oven, adding a few tablespoons of oil if the pot is dry, and sauté over medium to medium-high heat for 15 minutes, scraping up any brown bits, until the onions are tender and begin to brown. Add the garlic and cook for 2 minutes. Add the wine, beef stock, and thyme and cook for 3 minutes, scraping up any brown bits.

MAKE AHEAD
Refrigerate the cooked brisket and vegetables for up to 2 days. Slice the cold meat, put it back in the pan with the vegetables, cover with aluminum foil, and reheat in a 325-degree oven for 40 to 45 minutes.

Spoon half the onion and leek mixture under the brisket. Spread the tomato paste evenly on top of the brisket. Spoon the rest of the onions and leeks on top of the brisket, covering the tomato paste. Wrap the roasting pan tightly with heavy-duty aluminum foil. Roast for about 3½ hours, until the meat is extremely tender when tested with a meat fork.

Discard the thyme bundle and allow the meat to rest at room temperature for 15 minutes before slicing thickly across the grain. Serve the meat with the warm onion mixture spooned on top. Sprinkle with salt and serve hot.

lamb stew with spring vegetables

serves 6 to 8

When Jeffrey and I lived in Washington, D.C., I entertained at home a lot. Julia Child's wonderful lamb stew with spring vegetables was in my repertoire because I could make it in advance. This is my simplified version of that wonderful recipe.

2 tablespoons canola oil

¼ pound applewood smoked bacon, ¾-inch-diced

3 pounds boneless lamb shoulder, 1½-inch-diced (see note)
  Kosher salt and freshly ground black pepper

¼ cup plus 2 tablespoons all-purpose flour

2 tablespoons minced garlic (6 cloves)

2 cups canned beef stock, such as College Inn

1 cup full-bodied red wine, such as Côtes du Rhône, plus extra for serving

1 cup diced canned tomatoes, preferably San Marzano

2 teaspoons minced fresh thyme leaves

2 teaspoons minced fresh rosemary leaves

1 pound carrots, peeled and cut 2 inches thick diagonally

12 ounces small Yukon Gold potatoes, 1½-inch-diced

8 to 10 ounces fresh cipolline or pearl onions, peeled (see note)

6 small turnips, whole or halved, depending on size (1 pound)

2 tablespoons unsalted butter, at room temperature

1 (10-ounce) package frozen green peas, such as Birds Eye Garden Peas

½ cup chopped fresh parsley leaves

I prefer to buy one large piece of meat and dice the lamb myself to be sure the cubes are a consistent size.

To peel the onions, drop them in a pot of boiling water for 30 seconds, then trim and peel them, leaving the root intact.

Preheat the oven to 350 degrees.

Heat the canola oil in a medium (10- to 11-inch) ovenproof pot or Dutch oven, such as Le Creuset, over medium heat. Add the bacon and cook for 5 minutes, until browned. Transfer the

(recipe continues)

bacon to a large plate, leaving the fat in the pan. Dry the lamb with paper towels and toss it in a bowl first with 1 tablespoon salt and 1 teaspoon pepper, and then with the ¼ cup of flour. Raise the heat to medium high and cook half the lamb in the bacon fat for 5 minutes, turning occasionally, until browned. Add the lamb to the plate with the bacon and brown the second batch, also transferring it to the plate. Add the garlic to the pot and cook for one minute.

Pour the lamb and bacon, along with any juices that collect, back into the pot. Add the beef stock, wine, tomatoes (including the juice), thyme, rosemary, 2 teaspoons salt, and 1 teaspoon pepper and bring to a boil, scraping up the brown bits in the pot. Simmer for 5 minutes, cover, and place in the oven for 30 minutes. Add the carrots, potatoes, onions, and turnips, cover, and return to the oven for 1 hour, until all the vegetables are tender.

MAKE AHEAD
Prepare the stew through adding the flour-butter mixture and refrigerate. Reheat, add the peas and parsley, and serve hot.

Mash the 2 tablespoons of flour with the butter in a small bowl. Stir the mixture into the stew, and simmer on top of the stove for 3 minutes. Off the heat, stir in the peas and parsley, season to taste, and serve hot in large shallow bowls.

roasted vegetable paella

serves 6

There is an amazing professional cookware store in Paris called Dehillerin. Decades ago, I bought an enormous copper paella pan there and my sweet husband sat on the plane home with this huge pan on his lap! If you don't have a paella pan, you can certainly make this in a large Dutch oven.

2 pounds Holland bell peppers (red, yellow, and orange), cored, seeded, and cut into ½-inch-wide strips

2 pounds fennel bulbs, tops and cores removed, sliced ¼ inch thick

1 pound baby eggplants, unpeeled, sliced crosswise ¼ inch thick

1 large red onion, ¾-inch-diced

Good olive oil

Kosher salt and freshly ground black pepper

2 cups (¾-inch-diced) yellow onions (2 onions)

2 tablespoons minced garlic (6 cloves)

1 teaspoon saffron threads

1½ cups Spanish paella rice, such as Calasparra (see note)

1 (12-ounce) jar roasted red peppers, undrained, such as Mancini

1 teaspoon smoked paprika (not regular paprika)

5 to 6 cups simmering chicken stock, preferably homemade (page 68)

3 ounces freshly grated aged Manchego cheese (see note)

½ cup pitted Manzanilla or Cerignola olives, halved

½ cup thinly sliced scallions, white and green parts

You can buy Calasparra rice at Amazon.com.

Preheat the oven to 425 degrees. Position two racks evenly spaced in the oven.

Put the bell peppers, fennel, eggplants, and red onion in a large bowl, add ½ cup olive oil, 1 tablespoon salt, and 1 teaspoon black pepper, and toss. Divide the vegetables between two sheet pans and spread in one layer. Roast for 45 minutes, tossing occasionally.

I grate the Manchego cheese on a box grater; 12-month-aged Manchego has some of the flavor and texture of good Parmesan.

(recipe continues)

Meanwhile, heat 3 tablespoons of olive oil over medium heat in a 14- to 16-inch paella pan or large (11-inch) Dutch oven, such as Le Creuset. Add the yellow onions and sauté for 6 to 8 minutes, until tender. Add the garlic and saffron and cook for one minute. Add the rice and cook for 2 minutes, stirring to coat the rice with oil. Place the jarred peppers (including their liquid) and paprika in the bowl of a food processor fitted with the steel blade and process until pureed. Pour the mixture into the paella pan, stirring to combine, and bring to a boil. Add 1 cup of the hot stock and 2 teaspoons salt and cook uncovered over medium heat for 6 to 8 minutes, stirring occasionally, until the liquid is mostly absorbed, as you would cook risotto. Continue to cook the rice over medium heat for about 20 minutes, stirring in 1 cup of hot stock at a time whenever the liquid is absorbed, until the rice is al dente.

Add the vegetables to the paella, add one more cup of stock, and stir carefully. If the paella is dry, add more hot stock. Off the heat, stir in the Manchego cheese, olives, and scallions. Taste for seasonings and serve hot.

filet mignon with mustard & mushrooms

serves 4

When Jeffrey and I eat out in Paris, I love to order a classic filet of beef with mustard sauce. The rich beef and the creamy, spicy sauce are a great combination. This is my version of that dish, with some wild mushrooms added for even more flavor.

I make cracked black peppercorns with a mortar and pestle.

4 (2-inch-thick) filets mignons, tied (10 to 12 ounces each)
2 tablespoons canola oil
1½ tablespoons fleur de sel
2 teaspoons coarsely cracked black peppercorns
2 tablespoons unsalted butter
12 ounces cremini mushrooms, stemmed and sliced ¼ inch thick
2 tablespoons dry sherry
Kosher salt and freshly ground black pepper
1 tablespoon good olive oil
½ cup minced shallots (2 large shallots)
3 tablespoons Cognac or brandy
1¼ cups heavy cream
¼ cup Dijon mustard
½ teaspoon whole-grain mustard
2 tablespoons minced fresh parsley leaves

Preheat the oven to 400 degrees. Be sure your stove is well ventilated!

Heat a large (10-inch) cast-iron skillet over high heat for 5 to 7 minutes. Pat the filets dry with paper towels and brush all over with the canola oil. Combine the fleur de sel and cracked pepper on a small plate and roll the filets on the top, bottom, and sides in the seasoning, pressing lightly to coat. When the skillet is very hot, add the filets and sear evenly all over (top, bottom, and sides) for about 2 minutes per side.

Transfer the steaks from the skillet to a sheet pan (set the skillet aside) and place in the oven for 8 to 12 minutes, until the steaks register 120 degrees on a meat thermometer for medium rare. Remove from the oven, cover the sheet pan tightly with aluminum foil, and allow to rest for 10 minutes.

Meanwhile, heat the butter in a medium (10-inch) sauté pan over medium heat. Add the mushrooms and sauté for 4 to 5 minutes, until they release their juices. Stir in the sherry and cook for 10 to 12 minutes, until the mushrooms are cooked through. Sprinkle with ½ teaspoon kosher salt and ¼ teaspoon pepper and set aside.

At the same time, add the olive oil to the skillet (don't wipe it out), add the shallots, and cook over medium heat for 2 minutes. Add the Cognac, stirring to deglaze the skillet, and cook for 2 minutes, until the Cognac evaporates and the shallots are tender. Stir in the cream and simmer for 4 to 5 minutes, until thickened. Stir in the two mustards and taste for seasonings.

Remove the strings from the filets and place on 4 warm dinner plates. Spoon the mustard sauce around the filets. Spoon the mushrooms on top of the filets and sprinkle each plate with parsley. Serve hot.

roasted italian meatballs

makes 30 to 32 meatballs; serves 10

Traditionally, meatballs are fried in a pan until they're browned on all sides, but I've always hated the mess. Instead, I assemble these meatballs, put them on big sheet pans, brush them with olive oil, and roast them. Moist, delicious meatballs filled with Pecorino, Parmesan, garlic, and parsley and I don't have to clean the stove—or myself!—after they're done!

- 1 pound ground sirloin
- ½ pound ground pork
- ½ pound ground veal
- 1¾ cups dry seasoned bread crumbs
- ½ cup freshly ground Italian Pecorino cheese (2 ounces)
- ½ cup freshly ground Italian Parmesan cheese (2 ounces), plus extra for serving
- 2 garlic cloves, minced
- 2 tablespoons chopped fresh parsley leaves
  Kosher salt and freshly ground black pepper
- 2 extra-large eggs, lightly beaten
- ¾ cup dry red wine, such as Chianti
- ¼ cup good olive oil
- 2 (32-ounce) jars good marinara sauce, such as Rao's
  Creamy Parmesan Polenta (page 140) or cooked spaghetti, for serving

Preheat the oven to 400 degrees. Line two sheet pans with parchment paper.

Place the sirloin, pork, and veal in a large mixing bowl and lightly break up the meats with a fork and your fingertips. Add the bread crumbs, Pecorino, Parmesan, garlic, parsley, 2 teaspoons salt, and ½ teaspoon black pepper. Add the eggs, wine, and ¾ cup water and combine lightly but thoroughly.

Measure out 2-ounce portions of the mixture (I use a rounded 1¾-inch ice cream scoop) and roll each lightly into a ball. Place one inch apart on the prepared sheet pans. Brush the meatballs with the olive oil.

MAKE AHEAD
The meatballs can be made and roasted in advance and refrigerated for up to 3 days or frozen for up to 4 months. Heat the marinara sauce and reheat the meatballs in the sauce.

Bake the meatballs for 25 to 30 minutes, until lightly browned. Pour the marinara into a large pot and bring to a simmer. Carefully add the meatballs and simmer for 10 minutes, until heated through.

To serve with polenta, spoon a puddle of creamy Parmesan polenta on one side of each dinner plate. Spoon 1 or 2 meatballs plus a puddle of tomato sauce on the other side, allowing them to combine in the center of the plate. To serve with spaghetti, distribute among shallow pasta bowls. Spoon the meatballs and sauce onto the pasta. Sprinkle with extra Parmesan and serve hot.

orecchiette with farm stand pasta sauce

makes 2 quarts of sauce; serves 6

For a simple pasta dinner, there's nothing like homemade sauce that's slowly simmered with farm stand tomatoes, onion, celery, carrots, and garlic plus a splash of good red wine. This is a really satisfying sauce to make when the summer tomatoes are ripe and plentiful. I freeze it in quarts and serve it all winter.

5	pounds good red summer tomatoes
	Good olive oil
1½	cups chopped red onion
1½	cups medium-diced celery
1½	cups scrubbed and medium-diced carrots (2 to 4 carrots)
2	tablespoons minced garlic (6 cloves)
½	cup full-bodied red wine, such as Chianti or California Syrah
¼	cup tomato paste
½	cup chopped fresh basil leaves, lightly packed
¼	cup minced fresh parsley leaves
1	tablespoon sugar
½	teaspoon crushed red pepper flakes
	Kosher salt and freshly ground black pepper
1	pound orecchiette pasta, such as De Cecco
	Freshly grated Italian Pecorino and/or Parmesan cheese (see note)

Pecorino is saltier and sharper than Parmesan.

Bring a large pot of water to a full boil. Plunge the tomatoes into the water for 15 to 45 seconds (depending on their ripeness), drain, and immerse in a large bowl of cold water. Remove the cores and peel the tomatoes with a small paring knife. Cut the tomatoes into 1½-inch dice and set aside.

In a large heavy pot or Dutch oven, such as Le Creuset, heat ⅓ cup olive oil over medium heat. Add the onion and cook for 5 minutes. Add the celery and carrots, and cook, stirring often, for 10 to 12 minutes, until the vegetables are tender. Add the garlic and cook for one minute.

MAKE AHEAD
Prepare the pasta sauce and refrigerate for up to 5 days, or freeze for up to 4 months. Cook the pasta and finish the recipe.

Add the tomatoes, wine, tomato paste, basil, parsley, sugar, red pepper flakes, 1 tablespoon salt, and 1 teaspoon black pepper. Bring to a simmer, lower the heat, and cook, almost totally covered, for 1 hour, stirring occasionally. In batches, pour the sauce into a food processor fitted with the steel blade and pulse 2 to 3 times, until roughly chopped.

To serve, cook the orecchiette in a large pot of boiling salted water, following the directions on the package, and drain. Pour the pasta sauce into the pasta pot and reheat over medium heat, until simmering. Stir in the cooked pasta and 1 tablespoon salt and cook over medium heat for 5 to 10 minutes, until hot. Taste for seasonings and ladle into large, shallow pasta bowls. Sprinkle with Pecorino and/or Parmesan (I combine the two) and serve hot with extra cheese on the side.

rigatoni with sausage & fennel

serves 6

When it's cold outside, this is one of the heartiest and most satisfying dinners! I assemble it a day ahead, throw it in the oven to bake, and simply make a big green salad and buy some good crispy ciabatta.

3 tablespoons good olive oil

3 cups chopped fennel (1 large bulb)

1½ cups chopped yellow onion

1¼ pounds sweet Italian sausages, casings removed

2 teaspoons minced garlic (2 cloves)

½ teaspoon whole fennel seeds, crushed with a mortar and pestle

½ teaspoon crushed red pepper flakes

Kosher salt and freshly ground black pepper

1 cup dry white wine

1 cup heavy cream

⅔ cup half-and-half

2 tablespoons tomato paste

1 pound rigatoni, such as De Cecco

½ cup chopped fresh parsley leaves

1 cup freshly grated Italian Parmesan cheese, divided

Heat the olive oil in a large heavy pot or Dutch oven, such as Le Creuset, over medium heat. Add the fennel and onion and sauté for 7 minutes, stirring occasionally, until tender. Add the sausage and cook for 7 to 8 minutes, crumbling it with a fork, until nicely browned. Add the garlic, crushed fennel seeds, red pepper flakes, 2 teaspoons salt, and 1 teaspoon black pepper and cook for one minute. Pour in the wine, bring to a boil, and add the heavy cream, half-and-half, and tomato paste. Bring back to a boil, lower the heat, and simmer for 20 minutes, until the sauce has thickened.

Meanwhile, bring a large pot of water to a boil, add 2 tablespoons salt, and cook the rigatoni according to the directions on the package. Drain and add to the sauce, stirring to coat the

MAKE AHEAD
Spoon the pasta into gratin dishes, sprinkle with Parmesan, and refrigerate for up to a day. Bake for 20 minutes at 375 degrees.

pasta. Cook over low heat for 5 minutes to allow the pasta to absorb the sauce. Off the heat, stir in the parsley and ½ cup of the Parmesan. Serve hot in shallow bowls with the remaining ½ cup Parmesan on the side.

perfect poached lobster & corn
with tarragon butter

serves 4

A few years ago, I ordered a lobster from the seafood shop and ended up with the biggest lobster I'd ever seen! I had no idea how long to cook it. I came across Mark Bittman's instructions to cook it to an internal temperature of 140 degrees, regardless of size. How smart is that? I test meat with a thermometer, but it had never occurred to me to test a lobster!

Kosher salt
4 (1½-pound) lobsters (see note)
4 to 8 ears corn, shucked
12 tablespoons (1½ sticks) unsalted butter
1½ tablespoons roughly chopped fresh tarragon leaves
1½ teaspoons grated lemon zest (2 lemons)
Lobster crackers
Small bowls and small brushes for tarragon butter

I ask my fishmonger to kill the lobsters just before I take them home to cook them.

Fill a very large (18- to 20-quart) stockpot three-quarters full with water, add 2 tablespoons of salt, cover, and bring to a full rolling boil. Immerse the lobsters in the water and cook for 10 to 12 minutes, until an instant-read thermometer inserted into the middle of the underside of a tail registers 140 degrees. (Don't worry if the water doesn't come back to a boil.) Remove the lobsters with tongs, cover, and set aside.

Bring the water to a boil. Add the corn and cook for 5 to 10 minutes, depending on the starchiness of the corn, until tender. Remove with tongs.

Meanwhile, melt the butter in a small saucepan. Off the heat, stir in the tarragon, lemon zest, and 1½ teaspoons salt and keep warm.

To serve, slice the undersides of the tails lengthwise to allow people to take the meat out easily. Serve one lobster and one or two ears of corn per person plus a lobster cracker for the claws. Divide the warm butter among small bowls and give each person a small brush for brushing the butter on the corn.

roasted salmon tacos

serves 6

I love fish tacos but in place of the usual fried fish, I decided to fill mine with roasted salmon instead. It's not only more flavorful but there's no frying oil to deal with. I roast the salmon with a rub of chipotle chile powder, lime zest, and salt, and let everyone assemble their own tacos.

FOR THE SLAW

A mandoline makes slicing the cucumber easy.

¾ pound green cabbage, cored and finely shredded

½ seedless cucumber, unpeeled, halved lengthwise, seeds removed and very thinly sliced (see note)

¼ cup good white wine vinegar

3 tablespoons minced fresh dill

Kosher salt and freshly ground black pepper

FOR THE SALMON

Olive oil, for greasing the pan

1¾ pounds center-cut fresh salmon fillet, skin removed

2 teaspoons chipotle chile powder

1 teaspoon grated lime zest

Kosher salt and freshly ground black pepper

3 tablespoons freshly squeezed lime juice, divided

12 (6-inch) corn tortillas

4 ripe Hass avocados, seeded and peeled

¾ teaspoon Sriracha

At least an hour before you plan to serve the tacos, toss the cabbage, cucumber, vinegar, dill, 1 teaspoon salt, and ½ teaspoon black pepper together in a large bowl. Cover and refrigerate, allowing the cabbage to marinate.

These can also be served on one large platter or you can put out the components and allow each guest to assemble their own!

When ready to serve, preheat the oven to 425 degrees. Brush a baking dish with olive oil and place the salmon in it. Mix the chile powder, lime zest, and 1½ teaspoons salt in a small bowl. Brush the salmon with 1 tablespoon of the lime juice and sprinkle with the chipotle seasoning mixture. Roast for 12 to 15 minutes, depending on the thickness of the fish, until the salmon is just cooked through.

Wrap the tortillas in 2 foil packets and place them in the

oven with the salmon. Roughly mash the avocados with the remaining 2 tablespoons of lime juice, the Sriracha, 1 teaspoon salt, and ¼ teaspoon black pepper.

To serve, lay 2 warm tortillas on each of 6 plates. Place a dollop of the avocado mixture on one side of each tortilla, then some large chunks of salmon, and finally, some of the slaw. Fold the tortillas in half over the filling (they will be messy!) and serve warm.

MAKE AHEAD
Early in the day, prepare the slaw and season the salmon. Make the avocado mixture and place plastic wrap directly on top to keep it green. Cook the salmon just before serving.

fish & lobster cakes

makes 14 cakes; serves 6 to 8

Crab cakes are delicious but these fish cakes with a mixture of cod and lobster are much less expected. The creamy cod—with dill, lemon, and mustard—combined with chunks of sweet lobster meat, is wonderful. I ask the seafood shop to cook the lobster for me.

8 tablespoons (1 stick) unsalted butter, divided
1½ cups (¼- to ½-inch-diced) yellow onion
1 cup (¼- to ½-inch-diced) celery
1 large Holland red bell pepper, cored, seeded, and
  ¼- to ½-inch-diced
1¼ pounds boneless, skinless cod fillets, cut into 4 pieces
½ cup heavy cream
  Kosher salt and freshly ground black pepper
4 cups panko (Japanese bread flakes), divided
3 tablespoons minced fresh dill
2 tablespoons good mayonnaise, such as Hellmann's
1 tablespoon Dijon mustard
1 teaspoon grated lemon zest
2 extra-large eggs, lightly beaten
½ pound cooked lobster meat, ½-inch-diced
  Good olive oil
  Rémoulade Sauce (recipe follows)

Preheat the oven to 200 degrees.

Heat 3 tablespoons of the butter in a large (12-inch) sauté pan over medium-high heat. Add the onion, celery, and bell pepper and cook over medium heat for 8 to 10 minutes, stirring occasionally, until tender. Place the fish on top of the vegetables and add the cream, 1 teaspoon salt, and ½ teaspoon black pepper. Bring to a boil, lower the heat, cover, and simmer for 6 to 12 minutes (depending on the thickness of the cod), until the fish is just cooked. Set aside in the pan for 10 minutes, then flake the fish in large pieces with a fork.

Put 2 cups of the panko in a large bowl. Add the cod mixture,

If you prefer to cook the lobsters yourself, two (1½-pound) lobsters will yield ½ pound of cooked lobster meat.

MAKE AHEAD
Place the uncooked cakes on a sheet pan lined with parchment paper, wrap well, and refrigerate for a few hours. Sauté just before serving.

(recipe continues)

including the cooking liquid, the dill, mayonnaise, mustard, lemon zest, eggs, lobster, 2 teaspoons salt, and 1 teaspoon black pepper and mix gently.

Using a 2¼-inch ice cream scoop as a measure, shape the mixture into 14 (3-inch) fish cakes. Place the remaining 2 cups of panko on a plate and coat the cakes all over, patting the coating to adhere. Wipe the sauté pan clean with a paper towel and heat 2 tablespoons of the butter and 2 tablespoons of oil in the pan over medium heat. Place 5 cakes in the pan and cook for 5 minutes on each side, until nicely browned on both sides. Transfer the cakes to a sheet pan and keep them warm in the oven for up to 15 minutes. Repeat, adding more butter and oil, until the entire mixture is cooked. Serve hot with the rémoulade sauce.

rémoulade sauce

makes 1½ cups

1½ cups good mayonnaise, such as Hellmann's
6 tablespoons minced cornichons
1 tablespoon whole-grain mustard
3 tablespoons Champagne or white wine vinegar
Kosher salt and freshly ground black pepper

MAKE AHEAD
Prepare and refrigerate for up to 5 days.

Place the mayonnaise, cornichons, mustard, vinegar, 1½ teaspoons salt, and ¾ teaspoon pepper in the bowl of a food processor fitted with the steel blade. Pulse a few times until the cornichons are finely chopped (not pureed). Transfer to a sealed container and refrigerate.

shrimp & swordfish curry

serves 6 to 8

My late friend Anna Pump owned the specialty food store Loaves & Fishes in Bridgehampton, New York, for thirty-five years. I love everything she made, but this is Jeffrey's and my all-time favorite dish. It's a perfect winter stew, with shrimp, swordfish, and so many layers of flavor from onions, garlic, ginger, jalapeño, lime, curry, cumin, cayenne, and cloves.

1½ tablespoons curry powder
1 tablespoon ground coriander
1 teaspoon ground cumin
¼ teaspoon ground turmeric
⅛ teaspoon ground cayenne pepper
⅛ teaspoon ground cloves
4 tablespoons (½ stick) unsalted butter
2 tablespoons good olive oil
5 cups chopped yellow onions (4 onions)
1 Holland red bell pepper, cored, seeded, and cut into ¼-inch-thick strips
4 teaspoons minced garlic (4 cloves)
2 tablespoons grated, then minced, fresh ginger
1½ tablespoons seeded, minced jalapeño pepper
2 cups (16 ounces) canned diced plum tomatoes, including the juice
2 cups clam stock, such as Bar Harbor
Kosher salt and freshly ground black pepper
1½ pounds swordfish, skin removed and 1-inch-diced
1½ pounds (16- to 20-count) peeled and deveined shrimp (2 pounds in the shell)
Zest and juice of 1 lime

MAKE AHEAD
Prepare the sauce completely and refrigerate for up to a day. When ready to serve, bring to a boil, add the seafood, and finish as directed.

Combine the curry powder, coriander, cumin, turmeric, cayenne pepper, and cloves in a small bowl and set aside.

Heat the butter and oil in a large (11- to 12-inch) pot or Dutch oven, such as Le Creuset. Add the onions, bell pepper, garlic, ginger, and jalapeño pepper and cook over medium-low heat, stirring occasionally, for 15 minutes, until the vegetables are tender and starting to brown. Stir in the spice mixture and cook, stirring constantly, for 2 minutes. Stir in the tomatoes and the juice, clam stock, 1 tablespoon salt, and 1½ teaspoons black pepper, bring to a boil, lower the heat, and simmer for 10 minutes. Add the swordfish and shrimp, cover, and simmer for 7 minutes *only* (don't overcook the seafood!), until the shrimp and fish are just cooked through. Carefully stir in the lime zest and juice (don't break up the swordfish!), taste for seasonings, and serve hot.

crusty baked shells & cauliflower

serves 6 to 8

When I met David Tanis in Paris, he was the head chef at Alice Waters's legendary restaurant Chez Panisse in Berkeley, California. David now writes cookbooks and my favorite food column in the New York Times. *This wildly popular recipe is from his column. I love the creamy cauliflower with the crispy pasta plus sage, capers, garlic, and Fontina.*

Kosher salt and freshly ground black pepper
¾ pound medium shells, such as Barilla
Good olive oil
2½ pounds cauliflower, cut into small florets (1 large head)
3 tablespoons roughly chopped fresh sage leaves
2 tablespoons capers, drained
1 tablespoon minced garlic (3 cloves)
½ teaspoon grated lemon zest
¼ teaspoon crushed red pepper flakes
2 cups freshly grated Italian Fontina Val d'Aosta cheese, lightly packed (10 ounces with rind)
1 cup (8 ounces) fresh ricotta
½ cup panko (Japanese bread flakes)
6 tablespoons freshly grated Italian Pecorino cheese
2 tablespoons minced fresh parsley leaves

Grate (or rather grind) the Pecorino in the bowl of a food processor fitted with the steel blade.

Preheat the oven to 400 degrees.

Fill a large pot with water, add 2 tablespoons salt, and bring to a boil. Add the pasta and cook al dente, according to the instructions on the package. Since it will be baked later, don't overcook it! Drain and pour into a very large bowl.

Meanwhile, heat 3 tablespoons of olive oil in a large (12-inch) sauté pan over medium-high heat, add half the cauliflower in one layer, and sauté for 5 to 6 minutes, tossing occasionally, until the florets are lightly browned and tender. Pour the cauliflower, including the small bits, into the bowl with the pasta. Add 3 more tablespoons of oil to the sauté pan, add the remaining cauliflower, cook until browned and tender, and add to the bowl.

Add the sage, capers, garlic, lemon zest, red pepper flakes, 2 teaspoons salt, and 1 teaspoon black pepper to the bowl and stir carefully. Stir in the Fontina. Transfer half of the mixture to a 10 × 13 × 2-inch rectangular baking dish. Spoon rounded tablespoons of ricotta on the pasta and spoon the remaining pasta mixture on top. Combine the panko, Pecorino, parsley, and 1 tablespoon of olive oil in a small bowl and sprinkle it evenly on top. Bake for 25 to 30 minutes, until browned and crusty on top. Serve hot.

MAKE AHEAD
Assemble the dish, cover, and refrigerate. Bake before serving.

roasted ratatouille with polenta

serves 6

Ratatouille is a classic Provençal vegetable stew. I have always thought it would be interesting to roast the vegetables instead of simmering them. It turns out to be the perfect thing to pile on a big puddle of creamy Parmesan polenta. My friends love it!

It's not easy to cut round vegetables into cubes; I try to make them all similar sizes.

1½ pounds zucchini (6 to 8 inches long), ends trimmed and 1-inch-diced
1 pound eggplant, unpeeled and 1-inch-diced
1 Holland red bell pepper, cored, seeded, and 1-inch-diced
1 Holland yellow bell pepper, cored, seeded, and 1-inch-diced
1 red onion, halved and sliced ¼ inch thick
2 tablespoons minced garlic (6 cloves)
1½ teaspoons dried oregano
½ cup good olive oil
Kosher salt and freshly ground black pepper
15 cherry, grape, or small pear tomatoes, halved
¼ cup julienned fresh basil leaves
Creamy Parmesan Polenta (page 140)

Preheat the oven to 450 degrees.

Place the zucchini, eggplant, bell peppers, onion, garlic, oregano, olive oil, 1 tablespoon salt, and 1½ teaspoons black pepper in a large bowl and toss to combine. Pour the vegetables onto two sheet pans (if you put them on one pan, they will steam instead of roast!). Roast for 30 to 40 minutes, tossing occasionally, until the vegetables are tender and begin to brown.

Lower the oven to 425 degrees, add the tomatoes to the pans, and roast for another 12 to 15 minutes, until the tomatoes are tender. Add the basil and toss. Sprinkle with salt and serve hot over the polenta.

parmesan roasted zucchini

roasted vine tomatoes

root vegetable gratin

creamy parmesan polenta

tuscan roasted potatoes & lemon

couscous with pine nuts & mint

kasha varnishkes with wild mushrooms

italian white beans & escarole

vegetables & sides

fresh corn pancakes

herb & apple bread pudding

chipotle smashed sweet potatoes

tsimmes

spaghetti squash with garlic & parmesan

sautéed shredded brussels sprouts

roasted broccolini

New York Times
April 4, 1978

**CATERING, GOURMET
FOODS & CHEESE SHOPPE**
Shoppe. Top #1 loc w/unlimited poten-
tial. . All new equip & decor. In the
Hamptons. Gross over six figures in
summer alone. (914) 591-7263

the ad for the original store!

taking a chance

By the time I turned thirty I knew that cooking professionally was the something that was going to make me happy in life. One day I was sitting in my office in the White House, where I had a job writing policy papers on nuclear energy, reading the *New York Times*, and I happened to see a little section called "Business Opportunities." Among the listings for dry cleaners and delis for sale, I saw one for a specialty food store in a place I'd never been—the Hamptons. Specialty food stores, which sold fresh, homemade dishes that could be served at home, seemed to be popping up everywhere, as more and more women were entering the workforce and needed quick, convenient ways to make meals. I told Jeffrey about the ad in the paper, and to my complete surprise he said, "Let's go look at it this weekend!"

A few days later Jeffrey and I stood in front of a tiny specialty store in Westhampton Beach, New York. When I walked through the door for the first time, it truly felt like coming home. There was one person helping customers and another in the kitchen baking cookies, and I thought, "This is where I need to be." I made a low offer to buy the store and we drove home. The next day the owner called to say she'd accepted our offer. OMG, I just bought a business!

Two months later I found myself standing behind the counter on the Thursday before Memorial Day weekend. Diana, the former owner, was showing me how to cash out the register, and—I'll never forget this—we counted out exactly $85. For the entire day! Jeffrey, who had come up from his job working for Secretary of State Vance to help me for the weekend, multiplied $85 times the number of days in the summer and said anxiously, "I don't think you're going to make it." What we didn't know was that the next day (Friday of Memorial Day weekend) was a whole different story. When we closed the store that Friday at 10 p.m., there wasn't a single thing left in the store—not a cookie or a slice of cake or a pound of chicken salad. Nothing. And this was just the first day of a four-day weekend! That night Diana and I stayed up all night cooking. At about three in the morning I remember thinking that buying a store with no experience may have been the stupidest thing I'd ever done.

Instead of the elaborate food I used to cook for dinner parties, I learned that people wanted simple food at home. I taught myself how to simply roast vegetables, such as Roasted Broccolini (page 162) and Parmesan Roasted Zucchini (page 134). Not only did those ideas really help me run a successful specialty food store, but I use those recipes now and they're all in this book.

parmesan roasted zucchini

serves 6 to 8

Jeffrey adores zucchini with garlic and Parmesan. This is an easy recipe with lots of flavor and I love the texture of toasted panko on top. You can serve it hot out of the oven or at room temperature as part of a buffet, where a big platter of roasted zucchini looks gorgeous!

6 medium zucchini (2½ to 3 pounds total)

Good olive oil

Kosher salt and freshly ground black pepper

1 tablespoon minced garlic (3 cloves)

2 tablespoons minced fresh parsley leaves

2 tablespoons julienned fresh basil leaves

½ cup freshly grated Italian Parmesan cheese

¾ cup panko (Japanese bread flakes)

Preheat the oven to 425 degrees.

Trim the stem end of the zucchini, cut them in half lengthwise, and scoop out a small channel of seeds with a regular teaspoon. Place the zucchini in one layer on a sheet pan, brush generously all over with olive oil, and turn the zucchini cut side down. Sprinkle with 1 teaspoon salt and roast for 12 to 15 minutes, until just tender but still firm when tested with the tip of a small paring knife.

Meanwhile, make the bread crumbs. In a medium bowl, combine the garlic, parsley, basil, Parmesan, 1 teaspoon salt, and ½ teaspoon pepper. Add the panko and 3½ tablespoons of oil and mix well.

Turn the zucchini cut side up and spoon a heaping tablespoon of the panko mixture evenly on each zucchini. Bake for another 8 to 10 minutes, until the panko is crispy. Serve hot, warm, or at room temperature.

MAKE AHEAD
Prepare the zucchini and the crumb mixture separately and refrigerate for up to a day. Roast before serving.

roasted vine tomatoes

serves 6

If you need a quick vegetable for a dinner party, this is it! I roast cherry tomatoes right on the vine. They look great and it's one of those "toss with olive oil, salt, pepper, and into the oven" preparations that are not only easy to do but also really bring out the intrinsic sweetness of the tomatoes.

12 stems cherry tomatoes on the vine (3 to 4 pounds)
  Good olive oil
  Kosher salt and freshly ground black pepper
  Julienned fresh basil leaves, for garnish (optional)
  Fleur de sel

Preheat the oven to 350 degrees.

Place the tomatoes still on the vines (plus any that fall off the vines) on a sheet pan. Rub or brush gently with olive oil and sprinkle generously with kosher salt and pepper.

Roast for 10 to 15 minutes, until the tomatoes are tender and a few start to split. Sprinkle with basil, if using, and fleur de sel, and serve on the stem hot or warm.

root vegetable gratin

serves 8 to 10

I've played around with sweet potato gratins for years but because the potatoes have very little starch, the gratins don't bind—they end up as sliced sweet potatoes in cream. Instead, I decided to combine them with celery root for sweetness and Yukon Gold potatoes for starchiness and solved the problem deliciously.

Good olive oil

1½ cups sliced yellow onion (1 large)

2 cups (¼-inch-sliced) fennel, top and core removed

1 tablespoon minced garlic (3 cloves)

1 pound sweet potatoes, peeled and sliced ¼ inch thick

1 pound celery root, peeled and sliced ¼ inch thick

1 pound Yukon Gold potatoes, peeled and sliced ¼ inch thick

2½ cups heavy cream

½ cup chicken stock, preferably homemade (page 68)

2 cups grated Gruyère cheese (6 ounces with rind)

2 teaspoons minced fresh thyme leaves

Kosher salt and freshly ground black pepper

2½ cups coarse fresh bread crumbs, crusts removed

A mandoline makes short work of slicing potatoes. I use a knife for the celery root.

Preheat the oven to 350 degrees. Butter a 13 × 10 × 2½-inch oval baking dish.

Heat 2 tablespoons of olive oil in a large (12-inch) sauté pan over medium heat, add the onion and fennel, and cook for 10 minutes, tossing occasionally, until lightly browned and tender. Add the garlic and cook for one minute.

Meanwhile, in a large bowl, combine the onion mixture, sweet potatoes, celery root, Yukon Gold potatoes, cream, chicken stock, Gruyère, thyme, 1 tablespoon salt, and 1½ teaspoons pepper. Pour the mixture into the prepared baking dish and press lightly so the vegetables lie flat all the way to the edge. Combine the bread crumbs and 2 tablespoons of olive oil and distribute evenly on top. Bake uncovered for 1½ hours, until the vegetables are very tender when tested with a small knife and the top is browned and bubbly. Allow to set for 15 minutes and serve hot.

MAKE AHEAD
Assemble the dish, cover, and refrigerate for up to 24 hours. Bake before serving.

creamy parmesan polenta

serves 6 to 7

People often ask me what my go-to comfort food is and I have to say that this is it! I love the combination of creamy cornmeal, homemade chicken stock, and freshly grated Parmesan cheese. I pair it with Roasted Italian Meatballs (page 110) or Roasted Ratatouille (page 128) for a deeply satisfying winter dinner.

I use Bob's Red Mill medium-grind stone-ground cornmeal.

6 cups chicken stock, preferably homemade (page 68)
1 tablespoon minced garlic (3 cloves)
1½ cups stone-ground whole-grain cornmeal (see note)
Kosher salt and freshly ground black pepper
1½ cups freshly grated Italian Parmesan cheese
6 tablespoons crème fraîche
3 tablespoons unsalted butter, diced

Combine the chicken stock and garlic in a large saucepan and bring to a boil over high heat. Reduce the heat to a simmer and very slowly add the cornmeal, whisking constantly to make sure there are no lumps. Switch to a wooden spoon, add 1½ tablespoons salt and 2 teaspoons pepper, and simmer over very low heat for 5 to 10 minutes, stirring almost constantly, until thick. (The timing will depend on the cornmeal that you choose.) Be sure to scrape the bottom of the pan thoroughly while you're stirring. Off the heat, stir in the Parmesan, crème fraîche, and butter. Taste for seasonings and serve hot.

MAKE AHEAD
Prepare the polenta completely and refrigerate for up to 5 days. Spoon the polenta into a large saucepan with extra chicken stock or water and cook over low heat until smooth, creamy, and hot.

tuscan roasted potatoes & lemon

serves 6

One of my favorite restaurants in the world is London's River Café. It was started by Ruth Rogers and Rose Gray; their food is simple, modern, delicious Italian cuisine. Their potatoes roasted with lemon inspired this dish of potatoes, sliced lemons, garlic, and rosemary. I love all the burnt edges of the potatoes and lemons.

2 pounds Yukon Gold potatoes, unpeeled and 1-inch-diced

8 large garlic cloves, smashed and peeled (see note)

2 large or 4 small branches fresh rosemary

½ large lemon, cut in half through the stem and thinly sliced crosswise

3 tablespoons good olive oil

Kosher salt and freshly ground black pepper

Fleur de sel

Smash each garlic clove lightly with the side of a chef's knife to remove the peel, then smash it again.

Preheat the oven to 375 degrees.

Place the potatoes on a sheet pan, add the garlic, rosemary, lemon, olive oil, 2 teaspoons kosher salt, and 1 teaspoon pepper, and toss until everything is coated with oil. Spread out in one layer.

Roast for 50 to 60 minutes, turning the potatoes with a metal spatula every 20 minutes, until the potatoes are browned and crisp on the outside and tender inside. The garlic will be browned and sweet and the lemon slices will be caramelized. Discard the rosemary branches, sprinkle with fleur de sel, and serve hot.

couscous with pine nuts & mint

serves 6

Couscous is about as easy a dish as I can make, so I serve it often. Many people think it's a grain but it's actually like pasta—it's granular semolina that's precooked and dried so all you have to do is simmer some stock, stir in the couscous, cover, and let it sit for 10 minutes. Fresh mint and toasted pine nuts are really flavorful additions.

2 tablespoons good olive oil

1 tablespoon unsalted butter

1 cup chopped yellow onion

3 cups chicken stock, preferably homemade (page 68)

1½ cups couscous

  Kosher salt and freshly ground black pepper

½ cup julienned fresh mint leaves, loosely packed

⅓ cup pine nuts, toasted (see note)

Toast pine nuts in a dry sauté pan over low heat, tossing often, for 5 to 10 minutes.

Heat the oil and butter in a large saucepan over medium heat. Add the onion and cook over medium-low heat for 6 to 8 minutes, stirring occasionally, until tender but not browned. Add the stock and bring to a boil. Stir in the couscous, 1 teaspoon salt, and ½ teaspoon pepper and remove from the heat. Cover the pot tightly and allow the couscous to steam for 10 minutes. Fluff the couscous with a fork and stir in the mint and pine nuts. Taste for seasonings and add about 1 teaspoon salt, depending on the saltiness of the stock, and ½ teaspoon pepper. Serve hot.

MAKE AHEAD
Prepare the stock mixture and set aside. Ten minutes before serving, bring the mixture to a boil, add the couscous, and complete the recipe.

kasha varnishkes with wild mushrooms

serves 6

Jeffrey loves when I make traditional Jewish dishes. We made kasha varnishkes for years in the store for the holidays—it's buckwheat groats and bow-tie pasta—and anyone unfamiliar with the dish thought it tasted like the cardboard box the kasha came in! Not anymore: this recipe has sautéed shallots, wild mushrooms, and lots of fresh dill.

4 tablespoons duck fat, butter, or olive oil, divided
1 cup minced shallots (3 to 4 large shallots)
6 ounces cremini mushrooms, trimmed and sliced
1 extra-large egg, lightly beaten
¾ cup kasha (roasted buckwheat groats)
1½ cups canned beef stock, such as College Inn
Kosher salt and freshly ground black pepper
½ pound bow-tie pasta, such as De Cecco
1 tablespoon unsalted butter
¼ cup minced fresh dill

Heat 3 tablespoons of the duck fat in a large (8-inch) saucepan set over medium heat. Add the shallots and sauté for 6 to 8 minutes, until tender and beginning to brown. Add the mushrooms and sauté over medium-low heat for 5 minutes, until tender. Transfer to a bowl and set aside.

Meanwhile combine the egg and kasha in a bowl, making sure all the grains are coated with egg. Heat the remaining tablespoon of duck fat in the same saucepan, add the kasha, and cook, stirring almost constantly, for 3 to 4 minutes, until the grains are separated and dry. Add the shallot and mushroom mixture, the stock, 1 teaspoon salt, and ½ teaspoon pepper. Bring to a boil, reduce the heat, cover, and simmer for 8 to 10 minutes, until most of the liquid is absorbed and the kasha is cooked through.

Meanwhile, bring a large pot of water to a boil, add the pasta and 1 tablespoon salt, and cook according to the directions on the package. Reserve ½ cup of the pasta water and drain the pasta. Stir the pasta, butter, and dill into the kasha. Sprinkle with salt and add a splash of pasta water if the kasha is dry.

MAKE AHEAD
Prepare the dish completely, cover, and refrigerate. Add a little liquid and reheat in a saucepan on top of the stove.

italian white beans & escarole

serves 6

Lidey Heuck invited her friend Devon Elovitz to come for a tour of my vegetable garden. The three of us were talking about our favorite side dishes and Devon mentioned her mother's white beans and escarole, which they call Beans & Greens. It's both old-fashioned and modern. Thank you, Charlotte, I adore your recipe!

2 (15.5-ounce) cans white cannellini beans, preferably Goya
½ cup good olive oil
2 tablespoons minced garlic (6 cloves)
1½ cups good chicken stock, preferably homemade (page 68)
½ teaspoon crushed red pepper flakes
Kosher salt and freshly ground black pepper
1 large head escarole, leaves separated, trimmed, washed, and spun dry (see note)
1 cup freshly grated Italian Pecorino cheese
½ cup freshly grated Italian Parmesan cheese

Escarole is an old-fashioned Italian green that's available in the grocery store. I choose one that's between 1¼ and 1½ pounds.

Drain the beans, rinse, and drain again. In a large (11-inch) pot or Dutch oven, such as Le Creuset, heat the olive oil over medium heat, add the garlic, and cook for one minute, until the garlic is fragrant but not browned. Add the chicken stock, the drained beans, red pepper flakes, 2 teaspoons salt, and 1 teaspoon black pepper. Bring to a boil, lower the heat, and simmer uncovered for 5 minutes. With a potato masher or large spoon, mash half of the beans in the pot and simmer uncovered for 5 minutes.

Meanwhile, stack the escarole leaves on top of each other and cut them crosswise into 3-inch-wide strips. Add the greens to the pot, cover, and steam the greens over medium heat for 3 to 5 minutes, until tender, stirring the greens into the beans about halfway through. Off the heat, stir in the Pecorino and Parmesan cheeses, taste for seasonings, and serve warm.

MAKE AHEAD
This is delicious made early in the day, but it's best eaten the day it's made.

fresh corn pancakes

makes 20 to 22 pancakes

This is another recipe inspired by the wonderful New York Times *food writer David Tanis. When corn is plentiful at the farm stands in East Hampton, I love to make this. I combine fine and stone-ground cornmeal for the best texture. Buttermilk, sweet corn, and spicy Sriracha give these so much flavor!*

If your corn is starchy rather than tender, blanch the kernels in boiling water for 3 minutes and drain well before adding to the batter.

   1 cup fine yellow cornmeal, such as Quaker
   ½ cup stone-ground cornmeal, such as Bob's Red Mill
   ½ cup all-purpose flour
   2 teaspoons sugar
   2 teaspoons baking powder
   1 teaspoon baking soda
      Kosher salt
   1¾ cups buttermilk, shaken
   6 tablespoons (¾ stick) unsalted butter, melted
   2 extra-large eggs
   ½ teaspoon Sriracha
   3 cups fresh corn kernels (4 ears) (see note)
   3 tablespoons minced fresh chives, plus extra for serving
   1½ tablespoons seeded, minced jalapeño pepper
   8 tablespoons (1 stick) clarified butter, for frying (see note)

To make clarified butter, melt butter and pour it into a small measuring cup. When the milk solids settle, pour off the clear golden liquid and discard the rest.

Preheat the oven to 250 degrees. Line two sheet pans with parchment paper.

In a large bowl, stir together the fine and stone-ground cornmeals, the flour, sugar, baking powder, baking soda, and 1 tablespoon salt. In a medium bowl, whisk together the buttermilk, melted butter, eggs, and Sriracha. Stir in the corn, chives, and jalapeño pepper and mix into the dry ingredients with a rubber spatula until moistened. Don't overmix!

Heat 1 tablespoon of clarified butter in a large (12-inch) sauté pan over medium heat until it sizzles. Drop ¼-cup measures of batter into the pan without crowding them. Press each pancake very lightly with a small metal spatula. Cook for 2 minutes, turn, and cook for 1½ minutes, until both sides are browned

MAKE AHEAD
The batter may be prepared up to an hour ahead, covered, and allowed to sit at room temperature. Fry pancakes just before serving.

and the center of the pancake is firm. Place the pancakes on the
prepared sheet pans and keep them warm in the oven while
you cook the rest of the batter. Continue making the pancakes,
adding more clarified butter to the pan, as needed. Sprinkle
with salt and serve warm with a sprinkling of minced chives.

herb & apple bread pudding

serves 8 to 10

This bread pudding is based on the Thanksgiving stuffing that I've been making for Jeffrey for decades. I prefer to roast my turkey without stuffing because it cooks faster and stays moister. Bread pudding that bakes alongside the turkey is the best of both worlds: moist turkey and crispy stuffing.

8	cups (¾-inch-diced) country bread cubes, crusts removed
4	tablespoons (½ stick) unsalted butter
3	ounces pancetta, ½-inch-diced
2	cups chopped yellow onions (2 onions)
1½	cups medium-diced celery
1	Granny Smith apple, peeled and chopped
½	cup medium or dry sherry
2	tablespoons minced fresh rosemary leaves
	Kosher salt and freshly ground black pepper
½	cup chopped fresh parsley leaves
7	extra-large eggs
2½	cups heavy cream
1¼	cups chicken stock, preferably homemade (page 68)
2	cups grated Gruyère cheese, lightly packed (6 ounces with rind), divided

Preheat the oven to 350 degrees. Place the bread in a single layer on a sheet pan and bake for 20 minutes, tossing once, until lightly browned. Set aside.

Meanwhile, heat the butter in a large (12-inch) sauté pan over medium-low heat. Add the pancetta, raise the heat to medium, and cook for 5 minutes, until browned. Stir in the onions, celery, and apple and cook over medium to medium-high heat for 8 to 10 minutes, stirring occasionally, until the vegetables are tender. Stir in the sherry, rosemary, 1 tablespoon salt, and 1½ teaspoons pepper and cook over medium heat for 5 minutes, until most of the liquid is gone. Off the heat, stir in the parsley.

Meanwhile, whisk the eggs, cream, chicken stock, and 1½ cups of the Gruyère in a very large bowl. Stir in the bread and

MAKE AHEAD
Assemble early in the day, cover with plastic wrap, and refrigerate. Bake just before serving.

the vegetable mixture and set aside for 30 minutes to allow the bread to soak up the custard. Pour into a 9 × 13 × 2-inch oven-to-table baking dish. Sprinkle with the remaining ½ cup of Gruyère and bake for 50 to 60 minutes, until the top is browned and a knife inserted into the middle comes out clean. Serve hot.

chipotle smashed sweet potatoes

serves 8

One of my favorite restaurants in New York City is Jean-Georges Vongerichten's ABC Cocina. Jeffrey and I order lots of small plates to share and we always have a wonderful time! This is my version of their iconic sweet potatoes—they're spicy with chipotle peppers, sweet with maple syrup, and so creamy. It's a great way to shake up a Thanksgiving side dish!

4 pounds sweet potatoes (6 potatoes)
1 cup whole milk
1 cup heavy cream
1 tablespoon minced chipotle chiles in adobo sauce, with seeds, such as Goya (see note)
1 tablespoon adobo sauce (from the can of chiles)
¼ cup pure Grade A maple syrup
4 tablespoons (½ stick) unsalted butter, diced
Kosher salt and freshly ground black pepper

You can find cans of chipotle chiles in adobo sauce in the Latin section of the grocery store.

Preheat the oven to 350 degrees. Line a sheet pan with aluminum foil.

Place the sweet potatoes on the prepared sheet pan and pierce each potato 4 times with a small knife. Roast for 1 to 1¼ hours, until very tender inside when tested with a knife. Set aside until cool enough to handle. (Leave the oven on.) Peel the potatoes, discard the skins, and place the potatoes in the bowl of an electric mixer fitted with the paddle attachment.

Meanwhile, place the milk, cream, chipotle chile, and adobo sauce in a small saucepan. Bring to a boil, lower the heat, and simmer for 5 minutes. (It might look curdled.)

MAKE AHEAD
Prepare the sweet potato mixture, spoon it into the baking dish, cover, and refrigerate for up to 3 days. Bake at 350 degrees for 40 to 45 minutes, until hot.

With the mixer on low speed, add the chipotle-milk mixture to the sweet potatoes. Add the maple syrup, butter, and 1 tablespoon salt. Mix until the potatoes are coarsely pureed. Pour into a 9 × 12 × 2-inch oval oven-to-table baking dish and bake for 30 minutes, until heated through. Sprinkle with salt and pepper and serve hot.

tsimmes

serves 6 to 8

This traditional vegetable stew is often served on Jewish holidays. It has lots of orange vegetables—carrots, sweet potatoes, and butternut squash—slow-cooked with orange juice, brown sugar, cinnamon, and dried prunes. It's such a comforting side dish to serve with a brisket or roast chicken. And it doesn't need to be a holiday to make it!

Good olive oil
3 cups chopped yellow onions (2 large)
1 pound carrots, unpeeled and cut into 2-inch chunks
2 pounds sweet potatoes, peeled and cut into 1½-inch chunks
2 pounds butternut squash, peeled and cut into 1½-inch chunks
1 cup chicken stock, preferably homemade (page 68)
1 teaspoon grated orange zest
½ cup freshly squeezed orange juice (2 oranges)
¼ cup light brown sugar, lightly packed
2 tablespoons unsalted butter, diced
½ teaspoon ground cinnamon
Kosher salt and freshly ground black pepper
2 cups pitted prunes

Preheat the oven to 325 degrees.

In a large (10- to 11-inch) ovenproof pot or Dutch oven, such as Le Creuset, heat 2 tablespoons of olive oil, add the onions, and sauté over medium to medium-low heat for 15 minutes, stirring occasionally, until tender. Add the carrots, sweet potatoes, butternut squash, chicken stock, orange zest, orange juice, brown sugar, butter, cinnamon, 1 tablespoon salt, and 1½ teaspoons pepper and combine. Sprinkle the prunes on top and bring the liquid to a simmer on top of the stove.

Cover the pot and bake for 40 to 45 minutes, until all the vegetables are tender. Stir carefully, taste for seasonings, and serve hot or warm.

MAKE AHEAD
Prepare the entire dish and refrigerate for up to 2 days. Reheat on top of the stove before serving.

spaghetti squash
with garlic & parmesan

serves 5 to 6

A friend admitted to me that she wanted to like spaghetti squash but she found it too boring to eat. I said, "Try this recipe and see if I can change your mind!" You roast the squash with apple cider, shred it, and then sauté it with butter, garlic, Parmesan cheese, and parsley. Not even close to boring!

4 pounds spaghetti squash, halved and seeded (see note)
Good olive oil
¼ cup apple cider or apple juice
Kosher salt and freshly ground black pepper
2 tablespoons unsalted butter
2 teaspoons minced garlic (2 cloves)
¼ cup freshly grated Italian Parmesan cheese
2 tablespoons minced fresh parsley leaves

Preheat the oven to 400 degrees.

Place the spaghetti squash, cut sides up, on a sheet pan. Brush the flesh completely with olive oil and pour the apple cider into the cavities. Sprinkle with 2 teaspoons salt and 1 teaspoon pepper. Roast for 50 to 75 minutes, until the insides of the squash are very tender and shred easily when raked with a fork. It should be the consistency of al dente pasta. Set aside until cool enough to handle. Shred as much of the flesh of the squash as possible and transfer it to a large bowl. Discard the shells.

Heat 2 tablespoons of olive oil and the butter in a large (12-inch) sauté pan over medium heat until the butter starts to sizzle. Add the garlic and cook for just one minute, until fragrant. Immediately, add the shredded squash and sauté over medium heat, stirring occasionally, for 5 minutes, until heated through. Off the heat, stir in the Parmesan, parsley, 2 teaspoons salt, and ¾ teaspoon pepper. Taste for seasonings and serve hot.

To cut spaghetti squash, cut off the bottom with a large knife and stand the squash upright. Plunge the tip of the knife into the squash near the stem end and cut straight down to the bottom, being careful to keep your fingers out of the way. Cut the other side from stem to bottom and break the squash in half.

MAKE AHEAD
Roast and shred the squash, and refrigerate. Before serving, sauté the garlic, add the squash, and finish the recipe.

sautéed shredded brussels sprouts

serves 4 to 6

Jeffrey loves Brussels sprouts; not those mushy overboiled things our mothers used to make but rather sautéed or roasted Brussels sprouts that are flavorful and crispy. I decided to shred some sprouts like cole slaw and sauté them in a little butter. Instead of slicing the sprouts by hand, I put them through the feed tube of my food processor fitted with the slicing disk. Easiest Brussels sprouts ever!

2 (12-ounce) packages fresh Brussels sprouts, trimmed

2 tablespoons unsalted butter

2 tablespoons good olive oil

Kosher salt and freshly ground black pepper

1 tablespoon syrupy balsamic vinegar (see note)

There are many grades of balsamic vinegar. You want a very good, aged vinegar that is syrupy and almost sweet.

Place the Brussels sprouts in the feed tube of the food processor fitted with a large slicing disk. (You don't need to core them.) Process until they're all sliced.

Heat the butter and olive oil in a very large (12- to 14-inch) sauté pan over medium to medium-high heat. Add the Brussels sprouts, 1½ teaspoons salt, and ¾ teaspoon pepper and sauté, stirring occasionally, for 5 to 7 minutes, until crisp-tender and still bright green. Off the heat, stir in the balsamic vinegar, season to taste, and serve hot.

MAKE AHEAD
Prep the Brussels sprouts and place in a plastic bag with a damp paper towel for up to a day. Sauté before serving.

roasted broccolini

serves 5 to 6

Broccolini is a cross between broccoli and Chinese kale. Besides being a little more elegant, it's more interesting—sweeter and a little more peppery than regular broccoli. All you need to do is toss it with olive oil, salt, and pepper, toss it on a sheet pan, and roast it. Side dishes don't get any easier than this!

3 bunches broccolini
Good olive oil
Kosher salt and freshly ground black pepper

Preheat the oven to 375 degrees.

Trim 2 inches off the ends of the broccolini stems and discard. Cut any thick stalks in half lengthwise. Place the broccolini in a single layer on two sheet pans. (If you put them on one sheet pan, the broccolini will steam rather than roast.) Drizzle each sheet pan with 2 tablespoons olive oil, sprinkle with 1 teaspoon salt and ½ teaspoon pepper, and toss well. Roast for 15 minutes, until the broccolini is crisp-tender. Sprinkle lightly with salt and serve hot.

MAKE AHEAD
Prep the broccolini and store in a plastic bag with a damp paper towel. Roast before serving.

spiced pecans

fig & goat cheese bruschettas

challah with saffron

roasted plum chutney

herbed goat cheese

bread & cheese

port wine prunes with stilton
& walnuts

cherry pistachio biscotti

irish guinness brown bread

english oat crackers

warm vacherin

planning a party

The years that I owned my specialty food store, Barefoot Contessa, were wonderful years for Jeffrey and me. Jeffrey left the State Department in 1978 and moved to New York City to work as an investment banker, teach classes at New York University, and write for the *New York Times* and *Business Week*. Barefoot Contessa was only open during the summer months so I spent half the year running the store in Westhampton Beach and the other half catering private parties in New York City. But what I loved to do most was cook for Jeffrey and host dinner parties for our friends.

It was during this period that I really developed my entertaining chops. I made lots of mistakes but I also learned what makes a party really successful. Of course, it depends on the friends; I invite people who are going to show up and really have fun. But there are some subtle things that I found make a party more lively. I've talked about many of these details before but they're worth repeating. First, the simpler the dinner is, the more fun everyone has, including the host! Think about how you feel about sitting at a formal table with a million delicate glasses and a dinner that's plated restaurant-style, as opposed to big platters of fried chicken, baked beans, cole slaw, and cornbread placed right down the middle of the table family-style with everyone reaching over and helping themselves. Second, a 48-inch round table seating six people is ideal for a conversation that includes everyone. A long table usually breaks up into several conversations and you always feel that the other group is having more fun! Third, the music really sets the tone, so I choose upbeat music for cocktails, low-key music for dinner, and something more fun and lively at the end of the meal.

During those years, I also realized that the pacing of a dinner party is really important, too. In order to create a relaxed pace at a party, I always serve three courses and then maybe something like chocolates and a little glass of dessert wine at the end. But how do you serve three courses and not find yourself cooking all day?

For everyone who thinks I'm a relaxed cook, I don't want to disappoint you, but I'm totally *not*! I've learned to organize really well, to rely on recipes that are easy to prepare, and to serve lots of things that are assembled rather than cooked. For example, if I were serving the Skillet-Roasted Lemon Chicken (page 90) with Roasted Broccolini (page 162), that's two recipes I need to prepare the day of the party and that's enough for me! I make the second course really easy: a cheese platter that I can simply assemble. It looks gorgeous and inviting and it only takes me five minutes to prepare! For dessert, I might serve the Vanilla Rum Panna Cotta with Salted Caramel (page 198) that I prepared a day or two earlier and kept in the fridge. After all, entertaining isn't really about the food. It's about sharing a meal with people you love. It's what creates a community of people who care about and take care of each other. And that's really why I still go to the trouble of cooking for Jeffrey and my friends. It just makes me happy.

spiced pecans

makes 2 cups

David Lebovitz was the head chef at Chez Panisse, probably the most influential restaurant in the country over the past forty-five years. David now writes wonderful cookbooks, including The Perfect Scoop. *He makes spiced pecans to sprinkle on his homemade ice cream, but I also love to serve them on a cheese platter. My version of his pecans combines brown sugar, vanilla, cinnamon, ginger, chile powder, black pepper, and cloves. They're simply irresistible!*

Nonstick cooking spray or vegetable oil
2 tablespoons egg white (1 extra-large egg)
½ cup light brown sugar, lightly packed
2 teaspoons pure vanilla extract
2 teaspoons ground cinnamon
½ teaspoon ground ginger
½ teaspoon chile powder
¼ teaspoon ground cloves
Kosher salt and freshly ground black pepper
2 cups whole pecan halves (8 ounces)
½ teaspoon fleur de sel

Preheat the oven to 300 degrees. Spray a sheet pan with the cooking spray or brush it lightly with oil.

Place the egg white in a large bowl and whisk vigorously for 15 seconds, until light and frothy. Whisk in the brown sugar, vanilla, cinnamon, ginger, chile powder, cloves, 1 teaspoon kosher salt, and ½ teaspoon pepper. Add the pecans and mix well, until thoroughly coated. Pour the mixture, including any liquid, onto the prepared pan and spread in a single layer. Bake for 30 minutes, tossing twice with a metal spatula. Each time you toss the pecans, spread them out again in one layer. When they're done, sprinkle with fleur de sel and allow to cool completely; they will crisp as they cool. Serve at room temperature.

MAKE AHEAD
Cool completely and store at room temperature in an airtight container for up to 2 weeks.

fig & goat cheese bruschettas

serves 12

Jeffrey and I went to Provence with our dearest friends, Barbara and Bobby Liberman, who took us to the Bistrot de Mougins, one of their favorite restaurants. The owner, Alain Ballatore, kindly gave me the recipe for their famous fig tart, which inspired these fig preserves. OMG. It may be the best thing I've ever made! Whenever I serve it on a cheese board, my guests always insist on taking the leftovers home!

- 2 teaspoons grated orange zest (2 oranges)
- ½ cup freshly squeezed orange juice
- 3¾ cups sugar
- 1 vanilla bean, split lengthwise
- 2 pounds fresh ripe purple figs, stems removed and halved lengthwise
- 12 slices sourdough bread, for serving
- 8 ounces creamy goat cheese, such as Montrachet, for serving

Place the orange zest and orange juice in a medium (10-inch) heavy-bottomed pot or Dutch oven, such as Le Creuset. Add the sugar, vanilla bean, and figs to the pot. Cover and bring to a full boil over medium heat. (Don't worry; it may look dry.) Stir the mixture and boil hard for 1 minute, stirring to dissolve the sugar. Lower the heat, and cook uncovered at a full simmer for 50 minutes to 1 hour and 15 minutes, stirring occasionally. You want the little bubbles to be throughout the pot, not just at the edges. After 45 minutes, refrigerate a small amount of the liquid to see if it becomes syrupy. It should be like a soft fruit preserve. Keep cooking just until the liquid starts to gel when cold. If the liquid is too firm, add a little orange juice or water, cook for a minute, and test it again until it's right. Depending on how ripe the figs are, they will probably keep their shape, but it's fine if they don't. Discard the vanilla bean and serve or refrigerate.

Before serving, toast or grill the bread and spread with goat cheese. Spoon the fig preserves on top and serve.

MAKE AHEAD
The fig preserves can be prepared up to 2 weeks ahead and refrigerated. Toast the bread and assemble the bruschettas before serving.

challah with saffron

makes one large bread

One of the first things I ever made for Jeffrey after we were married was challah. It's a traditional braided Jewish egg bread similar to French brioche. I've added some saffron to give it a little heat. It's often served on Friday nights and important holidays.

1	cup warm (115 to 120 degrees) water
2	(¼-ounce) packages active dry yeast
½	cup sugar
¼	teaspoon saffron threads
3	extra-large eggs, at room temperature
1	extra-large egg yolk, at room temperature
5½	to 6 cups all-purpose flour
1	tablespoon kosher salt
¼	pound (1 stick) unsalted butter, diced, at room temperature
	Vegetable oil
1	extra-large egg beaten with 1 tablespoon water, for egg wash

Warm the bowl of an electric mixer fitted with the dough hook by rinsing it with hot water. Pour the warm water into the bowl (be sure it's at least 110 degrees when it's in the bowl), and mix in the yeast, sugar, and saffron. Allow to sit for 5 minutes, until it starts to froth, which tells you that the yeast is active. Add the eggs and egg yolk and mix on low speed. With the mixer on low, gradually add 4½ cups of the flour, scraping down the bowl as you go. With the mixer on low, add the salt and butter, then slowly add between 1 and 1½ more cups of the flour, mixing on low for about 5 minutes and continuing to add a dusting of flour to the bowl but only enough so the dough doesn't stick to the bottom of the bowl. The dough will be soft and a little sticky.

Turn the dough out onto a floured board and knead it by hand for a full 2 minutes. Roll the dough into a ball with the smooth side up. Brush a large bowl with vegetable oil and place

MAKE AHEAD
Bake the challah, cool completely, wrap tightly, and refrigerate for up to 3 days or freeze for up to 4 months.

(recipe continues)

the dough in the bowl, smooth side down. Roll the dough around to cover it with oil, then turn it smooth side up, making sure the entire dough is covered with oil to prevent a crust from forming. Cover the bowl with a clean, dry kitchen towel and allow to rise in a warm place for about 2 hours, until doubled in size.

Punch the dough down lightly and turn it out onto an unfloured cutting board. With a sharp knife, cut the dough into 4 equal pieces. Line a sheet pan with parchment paper. Turn the first ball of dough smooth side up and roll it into a cylinder. Roll the dough in a rope 17 inches long and lay it, seam side down, on the parchment paper. Repeat for the other 3 balls of dough, laying them side by side on the parchment paper.

To braid the dough, pile one end of the ropes on top of each other and pinch them together and under. With the pinched end away from you, take the far right rope and move it left over 2 ropes. Then take the far left rope and move it right over 2 ropes. Continue taking alternate ropes and laying them over 2 ropes until you've braided the entire bread. Pinch the ends together and fold them under. Cover the bread with a clean, dry kitchen towel and allow it to sit in a warm place for 45 to 60 minutes, until doubled in size.

Meanwhile, preheat the oven to 350 degrees. Place an oven rack in the lower third of the oven. Brush the bread thoroughly with the egg wash and bake for 35 to 40 minutes, until the outside is browned and it sounds hollow when you tap the bottom. Place the challah on a baking rack and cool completely.

roasted plum chutney

makes 2 cups

Cowgirl Creamery in Point Reyes Station, California, was started by Sue Conley and Peggy Smith and is one of the great cheese producers in this country. I particularly love their Mt Tam triple-cream cheese. Their cookbook, Cowgirl Creamery Cooks, *has a roasted plum chutney, which inspired this recipe. It's wonderful with cheese but also a perfect accompaniment to Cider-Roasted Pork Tenderloins (page 106).*

1 tablespoon good olive oil
¼ cup small-diced shallots (1 large)
1¼ pounds ripe red or purple plums, pits removed
    and cut into wedges
1 Granny Smith apple, peeled and ¼-inch-diced
¼ cup dark brown sugar, lightly packed
¼ cup freshly squeezed orange juice
2 tablespoons Port wine
1 (3-inch) cinnamon stick
2 whole star anise
⅛ teaspoon ground mace
¼ teaspoon kosher salt
    Cheese and crackers, for serving

Preheat the oven to 425 degrees.

Heat the oil in a medium (10-inch) ovenproof sauté pan over medium heat. Add the shallots and cook over medium-low heat for 5 minutes, stirring occasionally, until tender. Add the plums, apple, brown sugar, orange juice, Port, cinnamon, star anise, mace, and salt. Bring to a boil on top of the stove, place in the oven, and roast for 25 to 35 minutes, stirring occasionally, until the liquid is reduced and syrupy.

Remove from the oven and discard the star anise and cinnamon stick. (Be careful; I wrap a kitchen towel or oven mitt around the handle of the pan to remind myself that it's very hot!) Mash the fruit roughly with a dinner fork. Serve at room temperature or cold with cheese and crackers.

MAKE AHEAD
Prepare the chutney and refrigerate for up to 5 days.

herbed goat cheese

serves 8

When I was on my last book tour, I checked into a hotel and the chef kindly delivered a layered goat cheese and herb dish to my room. The layers of goat cheese, dill, basil, and red pepper flakes are so easy to make and it's delicious served on crackers with drinks.

2 **(6-ounce) creamy goat cheese disks, such as Coach Farm**
  Kosher salt and freshly ground black pepper
  Minced fresh dill
  Julienned fresh basil leaves
  Crushed red pepper flakes
  Good olive oil
  Bread or crackers, for serving

I use a Weck canning jar.

Find a small, wide-mouth canning jar or small glass vase (3½ inches in diameter by 4 inches high), just large enough to hold the two goat cheeses on top of each other with a little room to spare. Cut each cheese in half horizontally, making 2 rounds from each. (A piece of dental floss makes this easier.)

Place half of the first disk flat in the jar, sprinkle with salt and pepper, then with ½ teaspoon dill, 1 teaspoon basil, and a few red pepper flakes, and drizzle with ½ tablespoon olive oil. Place another disk of cheese on top and repeat the seasonings, herbs, and oil. Continue with the remaining cheese disks, piling one on top of the other with oil and seasonings in between. When all the disks are stacked and seasoned, drizzle 1 tablespoon of olive oil on top. Cover and set aside at room temperature for one hour or refrigerate for up to 24 hours. Serve at room temperature with bread or crackers for people to help themselves.

MAKE AHEAD
Assemble the jar and refrigerate for up to 24 hours. Serve at room temperature.

port wine prunes
with stilton & walnuts

serves 6 to 8

One of my favorite things to serve for a cheese course or dessert is English Stilton and a glass of Port wine. This recipe combines both of those flavors with sweet prunes, and they're a really surprising addition to any cheese board.

24 large pitted prunes

⅔ cup ruby Port wine

2½ ounces English Stilton, crumbled

2 tablespoons Italian mascarpone cheese

24 walnut halves, lightly toasted

Place the prunes in a saucepan just large enough to hold them in a single layer and add the Port. Bring to a boil, then lower the heat and simmer for 5 minutes. Remove from the heat, cover, and set aside for at least an hour for the prunes to become infused with the Port.

Meanwhile, in a small bowl, mash the Stilton and mascarpone together with a fork. Cover and refrigerate.

When ready to serve, place the slightly warm prunes on a serving platter, place a small mound of the cold Stilton mixture in the hollow of each prune, and top with a toasted walnut, pressing very lightly. Serve as part of a cheese platter.

MAKE AHEAD
Prepare the prunes and refrigerate for up to 4 days. Warm slightly, complete the recipe, and serve.

cherry pistachio biscotti

makes 25 to 30 biscotti

My friend Steven Barclay brought me some biscotti from Della Fattoria bakery in Sonoma County, California. I loved them so much that I called the owner, Kathleen Weber, to ask if she would share the recipe with me. There is something about the tender biscotti, sweet-tart dried cherries, and savory pistachios that makes this my favorite biscotti ever!

12 tablespoons (1½ sticks) unsalted butter, at room temperature

1 cup light brown sugar, lightly packed

½ cup granulated sugar

1½ teaspoons ground cinnamon

3 extra-large eggs, at room temperature, one separated

2 teaspoons pure vanilla extract

3 cups all-purpose flour

1⅓ cups almond meal or almond flour, such as Bob's Red Mill

1 teaspoon baking powder

½ teaspoon kosher salt

½ cup shelled pistachios

½ cup whole dried cherries

Turbinado sugar, such as Sugar in the Raw

Preheat the oven to 300 degrees. Line a sheet pan with parchment paper.

In the bowl of an electric mixer fitted with the paddle attachment, cream the butter, brown sugar, granulated sugar, and cinnamon on medium speed for 3 minutes, until light and fluffy. With the mixer on low, gradually add the 2 whole eggs, the egg yolk (reserve the egg white), and vanilla and mix until combined, scraping down the bowl with a rubber spatula.

In a medium bowl, combine the all-purpose flour, almond meal, baking powder, and salt. With the mixer on low, slowly add the dry mixture to the butter-sugar mixture, mixing only until combined. Scrape down the bowl and beater and make sure all the ingredients are combined. Stir in the pistachios and cherries.

Roll the dough into a ball on a well-floured board and cut in half. With floured hands, roll each piece into a cylinder about 11 inches long by 2 inches in diameter and place them 3 inches apart on the prepared sheet pan.

Place the reserved egg white in a bowl and beat with a whisk for 15 seconds. Brush the logs with the egg white (save the rest!) and sprinkle each with 1 teaspoon of turbinado sugar. Bake for 45 minutes, until lightly browned (the logs will be soft). Cool for 30 minutes.

Turn the oven down to 275 degrees.

Line two sheet pans with parchment paper. With a serrated knife, slice the biscotti ½ inch thick at a full 45-degree angle. Place the slices cut side up on the prepared sheet pans. Brush them with the egg white and sprinkle generously with turbinado sugar. Bake for 45 to 50 minutes, turning each slice once, until browned and fully baked. Transfer to a baking rack to cool.

MAKE AHEAD
Cool completely and store in a sealed container at room temperature for up to a week.

irish guinness brown bread

makes one loaf

Jeffrey and I spent a wonderful week in Ireland. Everyone was so friendly! I loved the brown bread that was served everywhere so I came home and did some research. The good news is that this bread is so easy to make— more like making a cake than a yeast bread.

1 cup quick-cooking oats (not instant), such as McCann's, plus extra for sprinkling

2¼ cups whole wheat flour, such as Heckers

¼ cup all-purpose flour

½ cup dark brown sugar, lightly packed

2¼ teaspoons baking soda

1 teaspoon baking powder

2 teaspoons kosher salt

1 (11- to 12-ounce) bottle Guinness extra stout beer, at room temperature

1 cup buttermilk, shaken

5 tablespoons unsalted butter, melted, plus extra for brushing the pan

1 teaspoon pure vanilla extract

Salted butter, such as Irish Kerrygold

Preheat the oven to 450 degrees.

In a large bowl, combine the oats, whole wheat flour, all-purpose flour, brown sugar, baking soda, baking powder, and salt. In a separate bowl, whisk together the beer, buttermilk, melted butter, and vanilla. Make a well in the dry ingredients and pour the wet ingredients into the well. With your fingers, stir the batter from the middle of the bowl to the outside, until it's well mixed. It will look more like cake batter than bread dough.

Brush a 9 × 5 × 2½-inch loaf pan with melted butter. Pour the batter into the pan and sprinkle the top with oats. Put the bread in the oven, immediately turn the temperature down to 400 degrees, and bake for 45 minutes, until a toothpick comes out clean. Turn the bread out onto a baking rack and allow to cool completely. Slice and serve with salted butter.

MAKE AHEAD
Cool completely and wrap well with plastic wrap. Store at room temperature for a day or refrigerate for up to 5 days.

english oat crackers

makes 24 crackers

Store-bought crackers are fine but there is something really special about homemade crackers. I love the chewy, nutty flavor of the old-fashioned oats plus a hint of brown sugar. These are particularly good with Cheddar and apples, or figs and blue cheese.

3 cups old-fashioned oats, such as Quaker
1 cup all-purpose flour
½ cup light brown sugar, lightly packed
1 teaspoon kosher salt
½ pound (2 sticks) cold unsalted butter, ½-inch-diced
¾ teaspoon baking soda
¼ cup lukewarm water
   Fleur de sel

Preheat the oven to 375 degrees. Line two sheet pans with parchment paper.

Place the oats, flour, brown sugar, and kosher salt in a food processor fitted with the steel blade and pulse for 45 to 60 seconds, until the oats are coarsely ground. Add the butter and pulse 15 to 20 times, until the butter is the size of peas.

Dissolve the baking soda in the lukewarm water and drizzle it over the crumbs in the food processor. Pulse until the mixture is evenly moistened and can be pressed into balls that will hold together.

With a 1¾-inch ice cream scoop or two spoons, scoop the dough into your hands and roll into round balls. Evenly space 12 balls on each of the prepared sheet pans. Flour the bottom of a flat-bottomed 3-inch-diameter drinking glass and use it to flatten each cracker so it is ⅛ inch thick and about 3 inches in diameter. The crackers will not be perfectly round. If there is a lot of flour on the crackers, turn them over with a metal spatula.

Sprinkle with the fleur de sel and bake for 20 to 25 minutes, until golden brown on the edges. Serve warm or at room temperature.

MAKE AHEAD
Prepare and store well wrapped at room temperature for up to 2 days.

warm vacherin

serves 8

Vacherin Mont d'Or is one of the most extraordinary of all French cheeses. When Jeffrey and I are in Paris for the holidays, every hostess serves it at her dinner party. A warm Vacherin is a particularly special treat for a cheese course when it's served with toasted breads and vinegary cornichons.

1 whole (16-ounce) ripe Vacherin Mont d'Or cheese, at room temperature (see note)
1 tablespoon good dry white wine
   Fleur de sel and freshly ground black pepper
   Good breads, thinly sliced and toasted
1 jar cornichons with pickled onions

Preheat the broiler and position a rack 8 to 9 inches below the heat.

If the Vacherin box is stapled together, simply place it on a sheet pan. If the box is glued together, wrap a piece of aluminum foil tightly around the bottom and sides (not the top) before placing it on a sheet pan. (Yes, you will be broiling the cheese in the box.) With a small sharp knife, remove and discard the top rind of the cheese. Pour the white wine over the cheese.

Broil the cheese for 2 to 3 minutes, watching carefully so the box doesn't catch on fire. Remove from the oven, sprinkle generously with fleur de sel and pepper, and serve immediately with toasted breads and cornichons. I put a small spoon in the cheese for people to help themselves.

This Vacherin is available only from September to May.

frozen mocha mousse

vanilla rum panna cotta
with salted caramel

pumpkin flan with maple caramel

raspberry rhubarb crostata

vanilla cream cheese pound cake

bourbon honey cake

dessert

apple pie bars

sparkling grapefruit granita

frozen mocha mousse

raspberry roasted applesauce

prune armagnac clafouti

devil's food cake
with coffee meringue buttercream

pecan rum raisin ice cream

chocolate crème brûlée

limoncello ricotta cheesecake

fresh peach cobbler

spicy hermit bars

frozen hot chocolate

apple pie bars

surprise them!

My late dear friend Anna Pump told me that no one remembers what you serve for dinner, but they always remember dessert! I tend to serve the main course buffet-style so people can choose what they want for dinner, but I never pass up the opportunity to get that "wow!" factor when I bring a fabulous dessert to the table. Guests always *say* they don't want dessert, but whenever I present a Devil's Food Cake with Coffee Meringue Buttercream (page 225) or pan of Limoncello Ricotta Cheesecake (page 232), everyone's eyes light up!

During the time that Jeffrey worked as an investment banker in New York, we often hosted dinner parties for his friends and colleagues. They probably expected a filet-of-beef-with-truffles kind of dinner but I prefer to surprise my guests. Even if I serve a fancy entree, I'm much more likely to end the meal with a very earthy dessert, something like Fresh Peach Cobbler (page 235) and a scoop of vanilla ice cream. One time I let each person assemble their own ice cream sundae. I'll never forget seeing a whole table of investment bankers take off their jackets and ties, roll up their sleeves, and dive into the M&M's and chocolate sauce like kids at a birthday party. I'm thinking they remember *that* dessert!

The other way I get that wow factor is by serving two or three different desserts. People simply go crazy. They might expect one showstopper dessert but they're certainly surprised to find two!

Secretly, I do this when I'm working on a book and I want to see if my friends prefer the Frozen Mocha Mousse (page 218) or the Raspberry Rhubarb Crostata (page 205), but I often make two desserts just for the fun of it. There is something so indulgent about it and it's all the more fun because it's such a surprise!

Going the unexpected route pretty much sums up my life. Someone once advised me to "complicate your professional life but not your personal life." How smart is that? The fact that my personal life is simple—and has been for almost fifty years—allows me the freedom to take the road less traveled. But at the end of the day, my greatest pleasure will always be cooking for my biggest fan, Jeffrey.

vanilla rum panna cotta
with salted caramel

serves 8

Since I discovered Fran's salted caramels, I've loved the combination of salt and caramel. I particularly like caramel with undertones of vanilla to balance the sweetness. Cold, silky panna cotta is perfect with warm, salty caramel. Make this panna cotta in advance and just heat the caramel and pour it on top before serving.

2 teaspoons (1 packet) unflavored gelatin
3 cups heavy cream, divided
2 cups plain whole-milk yogurt
2 teaspoons pure vanilla extract
   Seeds scraped from 1 vanilla bean
¾ cup sugar
   Dark rum, such as Mount Gay
½ cup good caramel sauce, such as Fran's
   Fleur de sel

I make vanilla extract by soaking vanilla beans in vodka.

In a small bowl, sprinkle the gelatin on 3 tablespoons of cold water. Stir and set aside for 10 minutes to allow the gelatin to dissolve.

Meanwhile, in a large bowl, whisk together 1½ cups of the cream, the yogurt, vanilla extract, and vanilla seeds. Heat the remaining 1½ cups of cream and the sugar in a small saucepan and bring to a simmer over medium heat. Off the heat, stir the softened gelatin into the hot cream until dissolved. Pour the hot cream–gelatin mixture into the cream-yogurt mixture and stir in 3 tablespoons of rum. Pour into 8 serving glasses and refrigerate uncovered until cold. When the panna cottas are thoroughly chilled, cover with plastic wrap and allow to chill overnight.

I use 12-ounce old-fashioned glasses from CB2.

Before serving, heat the caramel sauce with 2 teaspoons of rum in a small bowl in the microwave or a small saucepan set over low heat, just until warm. Spoon a thin layer of warm caramel on each cold panna cotta, sprinkle with fleur de sel, and serve.

pumpkin flan with maple caramel

serves 8 to 10

I like to include at least one holiday dessert in each book but there are just so many apple, pecan, and pumpkin pies you can make. I decided to take a different tack and make a flan—or custard—with all the flavors of a spicy pumpkin pie. The good news is that you don't have to make a pie crust!

FOR THE CARAMEL

- ¾ cup sugar
- ⅓ cup pure Grade A maple syrup
- ½ teaspoon fleur de sel

FOR THE PUMPKIN FLAN

- 1 (14-ounce) can sweetened condensed milk
- 1 (12-ounce) can evaporated milk
- 1 cup canned pumpkin puree (not pie filling)
- ½ cup (4 ounces) Italian mascarpone
- 4 extra-large eggs
- 1 teaspoon pure vanilla extract
- ½ teaspoon pure maple extract, such as Boyajian
- 2 teaspoons grated orange zest (2 oranges)
- 1½ teaspoons ground cinnamon
- ½ teaspoon ground nutmeg

Preheat the oven to 350 degrees.

For the caramel, combine the sugar, maple syrup, and ⅓ cup water in a small, deep, heavy-bottomed saucepan. Bring to a boil, swirling the pan (don't stir!) to dissolve the sugar. Cook at a low boil without stirring for 5 to 10 minutes, until the mixture turns a golden brown and registers 230 degrees on a candy thermometer. Watch it carefully so it doesn't burn! Off the heat, swirl in the fleur de sel, and immediately pour into an 8 × 2-inch round cake pan (not a springform!). Set aside to cool for 30 minutes.

Meanwhile, place the sweetened condensed milk, evaporated milk, canned pumpkin, and mascarpone in the bowl of an

MAKE AHEAD
The flan can be prepared and refrigerated in the pan for up to 3 days. Turn out just before serving.

(recipe continues)

electric mixer fitted with the whisk attachment and beat on medium-low speed until smooth. Whisk in the eggs, vanilla, maple extract, orange zest, cinnamon, and nutmeg. Gently pour the pumpkin mixture into the pan with the caramel so they don't combine.

Place the pan in a roasting pan large enough to hold the cake pan flat and fill the roasting pan with enough of the hottest tap water to come halfway up the sides of the cake pan. Bake in the center of the oven for 70 to 75 minutes, until the custard is just set. It will be firm but still jiggle slightly in the middle; a knife inserted into the center of the flan will come out clean. Remove the flan from the water bath, place on a cooling rack, and cool completely. Cover with plastic wrap and refrigerate for at least 3 hours. Don't tilt the pan or the caramel will run out!

Run a small knife around the edge of the flan. Turn a flat serving plate with a slight lip over the cake pan and flip them, turning the flan out onto the plate. The caramel should run out over the flan. Cut into wedges and serve with the caramel spooned over each slice.

raspberry rhubarb crostata

serves 6 to 8

My friends Johanne Killeen and George Germon from Al Forno restaurant in Providence, Rhode Island, introduced me to my first crostata, which is basically a rustic pie baked on a sheet pan. It can be filled with almost any fruit but this raspberry rhubarb crostata made my guests go berserk. This recipe makes enough pastry dough for two crostatas, so you can double the filling or save half of the dough for another time.

FOR THE PASTRY (MAKES 2)

- 2 cups all-purpose flour
- ¼ cup granulated sugar
- ½ teaspoon kosher salt
- ½ pound (2 sticks) very cold unsalted butter, ½-inch-diced
- ¼ cup ice water

FOR THE FILLING (MAKES 1)

- ¼ cup cornstarch
- 4 cups (½-inch-thick) sliced fresh rhubarb (1¼ pounds)
- 6 ounces fresh raspberries
- ⅔ cup granulated sugar
- 1 teaspoon grated orange zest
- ¼ cup freshly squeezed orange juice
- 1 extra-large egg beaten with 1 tablespoon water, for egg wash
- Turbinado or demerara sugar, such as Sugar in the Raw

Cut the stalks of rhubarb crosswise.

For the pastry, place the flour, granulated sugar, and salt in the bowl of a food processor fitted with the steel blade. Pulse a few times to combine. Add the butter and toss carefully with your fingers to coat each cube of butter with the flour. Pulse 12 to 15 times, or until the butter is the size of peas. With the motor running, add the ice water all at once through the feed tube. Keep hitting the pulse button just until the dough comes together. Turn onto a well-floured board, cut in half, and form into two disks. Wrap and refrigerate for at least an hour. (Wrap the second dough well and freeze, if not using.)

If the dough is refrigerated for more than an hour, let it rest at room temperature for 15 minutes before rolling it out.

(recipe continues)

For the filling, place 3 tablespoons of water in small bowl, whisk in the cornstarch, and set aside. In a large heavy-bottomed saucepan, combine the rhubarb, raspberries, granulated sugar, orange zest, and orange juice. Cook over medium heat for 5 to 6 minutes, until some of the juices are released. Stir in the cornstarch, bring to a boil, lower the heat, and simmer for 2 minutes. Refrigerate for 30 minutes, until cool.

Preheat the oven to 425 degrees. Line a sheet pan with parchment paper.

Roll the pastry into an 11- to 12-inch circle on a lightly floured surface and transfer to the prepared pan. Pile the raspberry rhubarb mixture onto the pastry, leaving a 1½-inch border all around. Fold the border up over the filling, pleating if necessary and pressing lightly. Brush the pastry with egg wash, sprinkle just the pastry with turbinado sugar, and bake for 30 to 35 minutes, until the pastry is browned and the filling is thickened. Cool for 30 minutes and serve warm or at room temperature.

vanilla cream cheese pound cake

makes 2 loaves

I have a total weakness for any kind of pound cake. This one has the perfect moist, dense texture from cake flour instead of all-purpose flour, and the deep vanilla flavor comes from both vanilla extract and the seeds of a vanilla bean. Nothing says "Welcome home" more than the smell of freshly baked cake!

Baking spray with flour, such as Baker's Joy

3 tablespoons demerara or turbinado sugar, such as Sugar in the Raw

¾ pound (3 sticks) unsalted butter, at room temperature

8 ounces cream cheese, at room temperature

2½ cups granulated sugar

6 extra-large eggs, at room temperature

1 tablespoon pure vanilla extract

Seeds scraped from 1 vanilla bean

3 cups sifted cake flour (measured after sifting)

1 teaspoon kosher salt

Test your oven with an oven thermometer to be sure it's accurate!

Preheat the oven to 325 degrees. Spray two 8½ × 4½ × 2½-inch metal loaf pans with the baking spray and sprinkle the insides of the pans with the demerara sugar, tilting the pans to cover evenly.

Place the butter, cream cheese, and granulated sugar in the bowl of an electric mixer fitted with the paddle attachment and beat on medium speed for 2½ to 3 minutes, until light and creamy. Scrape down the bowl with a rubber spatula to be sure it's well mixed. With the mixer on low, add the eggs, one at a time, mixing well and scraping down the bowl before adding the next egg. Mix in the vanilla extract and vanilla seeds.

Combine the cake flour and salt in a medium bowl. With the mixer on low, slowly add the flour mixture to the butter mixture, scraping down the bowl and beater with a rubber spatula. Mix the batter with the spatula to be sure it's well mixed. Divide

MAKE AHEAD Wrap the cakes well and refrigerate for up to 3 days or freeze for up to 3 months. Serve at room temperature.

the batter evenly between the two loaf pans, smooth the tops, and bake in the center of the oven for 60 to 70 minutes, until a toothpick inserted into the center of each cake comes out clean.

Allow the cakes to cool in the pans for 30 minutes, then carefully turn them out and cool completely on a baking rack.

bourbon honey cake

serves 12 to 16

Honey cake is a classic Jewish holiday dessert; I like it moist, spicy, and topped with toasted almonds. Mine has layers and layers of subtle flavor from honey, brown sugar, orange zest, coffee, and spices like cinnamon, cloves, allspice, and ginger. How good does that sound? Oh! And one more thing: bourbon! Jeffrey loves this cake.

1 cup vegetable oil, plus extra for the pan

3¾ cups all-purpose flour, plus extra for the pan

1½ cups granulated sugar

1 cup honey

½ cup light brown sugar, lightly packed

3 extra-large eggs, at room temperature

2 teaspoons grated orange zest (2 oranges)

1 teaspoon pure vanilla extract

1 tablespoon baking powder

1 teaspoon baking soda

4 teaspoons ground cinnamon

1 teaspoon kosher salt

½ teaspoon ground cloves

½ teaspoon ground allspice

½ teaspoon ground ginger

1 cup hot coffee

½ cup freshly squeezed orange juice (2 oranges)

¼ cup good bourbon, such as Maker's Mark

½ cup blanched sliced almonds

To be sure the eggs are at room temperature, I leave them out overnight.

MAKE AHEAD
Prepare the cake completely, wrap tightly in plastic wrap, and store at room temperature for one day, refrigerate for up to 4 days, or freeze for up to 4 months.

Preheat the oven to 350 degrees. Brush a 9-inch angel food cake pan with a nonremovable bottom with oil, line the bottom with parchment paper, then oil and flour the pan.

In the bowl of an electric mixer fitted with the paddle attachment, mix the oil, granulated sugar, honey, brown sugar, eggs, orange zest, and vanilla on medium speed for one minute. In another bowl, sift together the flour, baking powder, baking soda, cinnamon, salt, cloves, allspice, and ginger and blend.

(recipe continues)

Combine the coffee, orange juice, and bourbon in a 2-cup glass measuring cup. With the mixer on low, alternately add the flour and liquid mixtures to the oil-sugar mixture in thirds, beginning and ending with flour, until combined. Scrape down the bowl with a rubber spatula. Don't worry; the batter will be very liquid!

Pour the batter into the prepared pan. Rap the pan 5 times on the counter to get rid of any bubbles in the batter. Sprinkle the top with the almonds. Bake in the center of the oven for 40 to 45 minutes, until a toothpick inserted into the center comes out clean. Cool completely, then remove from the pan and place almond side up on a flat serving plate. Serve at room temperature.

sweetened whipped cream

serves 4

    1 cup cold heavy cream (8 ounces)
2½ tablespoons sugar
    1 teaspoon pure vanilla extract

Place the cream, sugar, and vanilla in the bowl of an electric mixer fitted with the whisk attachment and beat on high speed until the cream forms very soft peaks (don't overbeat or the cream will be too firm).

apple pie bars

makes 12 bars

When I bought my specialty food store, Barefoot Contessa, Jeffrey took me on a grand tour of food stores in California looking for inspiration, including a visit to the iconic Oakville Grocery in Napa Valley. I was there again recently and they were making apple pie bars—what a great idea! I worked on my version of the bars with two kinds of apples, tart Granny Smiths and sweet Golden Delicious. One large batch of buttery shortbread makes both the crust and the crumble topping.

FOR THE CRUST

    1 pound (4 sticks) unsalted butter, at room temperature

    ¾ cup granulated sugar

    ½ cup light brown sugar, lightly packed

    2 teaspoons pure vanilla extract

    4 cups all-purpose flour

    1½ teaspoons kosher salt

    ½ cup chopped walnuts

    1 teaspoon ground cinnamon

FOR THE APPLE FILLING

    1½ pounds Granny Smith apples, peeled, quartered, cored, and sliced ⅛ inch thick (3 large)

    1½ pounds Golden Delicious apples, peeled, quartered, cored, and sliced ⅛ inch thick (3 large)

    2 tablespoons freshly squeezed lemon juice

    ¼ cup granulated sugar

    1 teaspoon ground cinnamon

    ⅛ teaspoon ground nutmeg

    4 tablespoons (½ stick) unsalted butter

Preheat the oven to 375 degrees.

For the crust, place the butter, granulated sugar, brown sugar, and vanilla in the bowl of an electric mixer fitted with the paddle attachment and beat on medium speed for 2 minutes, until light and creamy. Sift the flour and salt together and, with the mixer on low, slowly add to the butter-sugar mixture, beating until combined. Scatter two-thirds of the dough in

MAKE AHEAD
Bake, cool completely, wrap tightly, and store at room temperature for up to 2 days.

clumps in a 9 × 13-inch baking pan and press it lightly with floured hands on the bottom and ½ inch up the sides (see note). Refrigerate for 20 minutes. Bake for 18 to 20 minutes, until the crust is golden brown, and set aside to cool.

Meanwhile, put the mixing bowl with the remaining dough back on the mixer, add the walnuts and cinnamon, and mix on low speed to combine. Set aside.

Reduce the oven to 350 degrees.

For the filling, combine the Granny Smith and Golden Delicious apples and lemon juice in a very large bowl. Add the granulated sugar, cinnamon, and nutmeg and mix well. Melt the butter in a large (10-inch-diameter) pot, add the apples, and simmer over medium to medium-low heat, stirring often, for 12 to 15 minutes, until the apples are tender and the liquid has mostly evaporated. Spread the apples evenly over the crust, leaving a ½-inch border.

Pinch medium pieces of the remaining dough with your fingers and drop them evenly on top of the apples (they will not be covered). Bake for 25 to 30 minutes, until the topping is browned. Cool completely and cut into bars.

Use a metal measuring cup to make the corners.

sparkling grapefruit granita

serves 6 to 8

I often serve a cheese course before dessert so I'm looking for something light and refreshing like a granita to serve afterward. I make the mixture in advance and then freeze it a few hours before dinner. This granita combines freshly squeezed grapefruit juice, rosé Champagne, and just a pinch of salt. It's a very elegant dessert after a special dinner.

1 cup sugar

2 cups freshly squeezed pink grapefruit juice
(3 to 4 large grapefruits)

2 cups dry rosé Champagne

⅛ teaspoon fleur de sel

Combine the sugar with 1 cup water in a small saucepan. Bring to a boil and simmer for 2 minutes, until the sugar dissolves. Pour into a 9 × 13 × 2-inch rectangular (non-metal) baking dish. Stir in the grapefruit juice, Champagne, and fleur de sel.

Carefully place the dish on a level surface in the freezer. Freeze for one hour, rake the granita with a large dinner fork, and return it to the freezer. Continue to rake the granita every 30 minutes, until it's firm and granular. This might take as long as 3 hours. Serve frozen in pretty bowls or stemmed glasses.

MAKE AHEAD
Prepare the recipe 3 to 6 hours in advance, wrap tightly, and store in the freezer. Scrape with a fork before serving.

frozen mocha mousse

serves 8

At Barefoot Contessa, we used to make a lot of frozen desserts. This mocha mousse was always our best seller! The combination of bittersweet chocolate, Kahlúa, cocoa powder, and espresso is amazing.

7 ounces bittersweet chocolate, such as Lindt, divided
3 tablespoons coffee liqueur, such as Kahlúa
6 extra-large eggs, separated, at room temperature
¾ cup sugar
¼ cup unsweetened cocoa powder, such as Pernigotti
2 teaspoons instant espresso granules
1 teaspoon pure vanilla extract
　Pinch of kosher salt
2 cups cold heavy cream
　Sweetened Whipped Cream (page 213)
　Grated bittersweet chocolate, for garnish

Place 3 ounces of the chocolate, the coffee liqueur, and 3 tablespoons of water in a small bowl and cover with plastic wrap. Heat the mixture in the microwave for 30 seconds, stir, then heat for another 15 seconds, continuing just until the chocolate melts. Stir until smooth and set aside to cool.

Place the egg yolks and sugar in the bowl of an electric mixer fitted with the paddle attachment and beat on medium speed for 3 minutes, until the mixture is thick like mayonnaise. With the mixer on low, add the cooled chocolate mixture, the cocoa powder, espresso, and vanilla.

Place the egg whites and salt in a clean, dry mixing bowl fitted with the whisk attachment and beat on high speed until the whites form soft (not dry!) peaks. Carefully fold into the chocolate mixture with a rubber spatula. In the same bowl (no need to clean it!), beat the cream on high speed until it forms soft peaks, then fold it into the chocolate mixture. Grate the remaining 4 ounces of chocolate (see note) and fold it into the mousse with a rubber spatula.

Pour the mixture into a 10-cup soufflé dish, cover, and freeze for several hours or overnight. Before serving, pipe the edge of the mousse with sweetened whipped cream and sprinkle with extra grated chocolate. Serve frozen with extra whipped cream on the side.

You can grate chocolate either by hand or in a food processor fitted with the carrot grating disk.

MAKE AHEAD
Prepare the mousse, wrap well, and freeze for up to 1 month.

raspberry roasted applesauce

makes 2½ quarts; serves 8

A scoop of cold vanilla ice cream melting into a bowl of warm homemade applesauce is my idea of heaven. When local farm stands finally have apples in the fall, I make all kinds of fresh applesauce. For this raspberry applesauce, peel the apples (I combine tart Granny Smiths with sweet Macouns) and throw them in a Dutch oven with orange juice, lemon juice, and fresh raspberries—an hour later you have fresh raspberry applesauce.

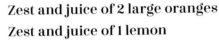

Zest and juice of 2 large oranges
Zest and juice of 1 lemon
3 pounds Granny Smith apples (6 to 8 apples)
3 pounds sweet red apples, such as Macoun (6 to 8 apples)
½ cup light brown sugar, lightly packed
4 tablespoons (½ stick) unsalted butter
2 teaspoons ground cinnamon
12 ounces fresh raspberries (2 packages)
Vanilla ice cream, such as Häagen-Dazs, for serving
Orange zest, for serving

I use a strip zester when I cook the applesauce and either a strip zester or rasp for the garnish.

Preheat the oven to 350 degrees.

Place the zest and juice of the oranges and lemon in a large (11-inch) ovenproof pot or Dutch oven, such as Le Creuset. Peel, quarter, and core the apples and add them to the pot, tossing them with the juices as you go.

Add the brown sugar, butter, cinnamon, and raspberries, cover, and bake for 1 to 1¼ hours, until the apples are very soft. Stir vigorously with a wire whisk. The applesauce will be smooth but still have a lot of texture. Serve warm with a scoop of ice cream and a dusting of orange zest.

MAKE AHEAD
Applesauce can be prepared and refrigerated for up to 5 days. Serve cold or warm.

prune armagnac clafouti

serves 8

Clafouti is a pancake-like batter poured over fruit and baked. I like to serve it slightly warm right out of the oven. Traditionally, it's made with cherries but this one has Armagnac and prunes, and it's a great combination!

1 tablespoon unsalted butter, at room temperature
Granulated sugar
1 cup pitted prunes, ½-inch-diced (6 ounces)
Good Armagnac
3 extra-large eggs, at room temperature
6 tablespoons all-purpose flour
½ teaspoon baking powder
¼ teaspoon kosher salt
1½ cups heavy cream
2 teaspoons pure vanilla extract
1 teaspoon grated lemon zest
Confectioners' sugar, for dusting

Preheat the oven to 375 degrees. Grease a 10 × 1½-inch round baking dish with the butter and sprinkle with 1 tablespoon of granulated sugar.

In a small bowl, combine the prunes with 2 tablespoons of Armagnac and microwave on high for 1 minute. Set aside.

In the bowl of an electric mixer fitted with the paddle attachment, beat the eggs and ⅓ cup granulated sugar on medium-high speed for 3 minutes, until light and thick. In a small bowl, combine the flour, baking powder, and salt. Combine the cream, vanilla, lemon zest, and 1 tablespoon Armagnac in a glass measuring cup. On low speed, slowly add the dry ingredients to the batter and then add the liquid ingredients, mixing well. Set aside for 10 minutes.

Distribute the prunes in the prepared pan and carefully pour on the batter. Sprinkle evenly with 1 teaspoon granulated sugar. Bake for 35 to 40 minutes, until the top is golden brown and a toothpick comes out clean. Cool slightly, sprinkle with confectioners' sugar, and serve warm.

MAKE AHEAD
Prepare the batter and refrigerate. Soak the prunes and refrigerate. Assemble the clafouti and bake just before serving.

devil's food cake
with coffee meringue buttercream

makes one 9-inch 4-layer cake; serves 12 to 16

This cake is a showstopper! I bake the cakes one day and make the butter-cream and assemble the cakes the next so it is not too daunting. I adore the combination of moist chocolate cake and lighter-than-air buttercream.

¾	pound (3 sticks) unsalted butter, at room temperature
2¼	cups sugar
4	extra-large eggs, at room temperature
4	teaspoons pure vanilla extract
¾	cup unsweetened cocoa powder, such as Pernigotti
¾	cup hot brewed coffee or espresso
3	cups all-purpose flour
1	teaspoon baking soda
1	teaspoon baking powder
1½	teaspoons kosher salt
1	cup sour cream
	Coffee Meringue Buttercream (recipe follows)
	Chocolate espresso beans, for decoration

Preheat the oven to 350 degrees. Grease two 9 × 2-inch round cake pans, line them with parchment paper, then grease and flour the pans. Set aside.

In the bowl of an electric mixer fitted with the paddle attachment, cream the butter and sugar on medium speed for 3 minutes, until light and fluffy. On low speed, add the eggs, one at a time. Add the vanilla and beat until well mixed, scraping down the bowl with a rubber spatula.

Whisk the cocoa powder and hot coffee together in a small bowl. With the mixer on low, add it into the batter.

In a medium bowl, sift together the flour, baking soda, baking powder, and salt. With the mixer on low, slowly add half the flour mixture to the batter, then all the sour cream, then the remaining flour mixture, mixing each addition until combined. With a rubber spatula, fold the batter until it is well mixed.

(recipe continues)

MAKE AHEAD
Bake and frost the cake completely, cover with plastic wrap, and refrigerate for up to 3 days. Serve at room temperature.

Divide the batter equally between the two prepared pans and smooth the tops. Bake for 30 to 35 minutes, until a toothpick inserted into the center comes out clean. Cool in the pans for 30 minutes, turn out onto a baking rack, and cool completely.

To frost the cakes, slice them in half horizontally with a long, thin knife (see note). Place the bottom of the first cake, cut side up, on a flat serving plate and spread a thin layer of buttercream on the top only (not the sides) with a palette knife. Place the top of the first cake, cut side down, on top and thinly frost the top only. Next, place the top layer of the second cake on top, cut side up, and thinly frost. Finally, place the bottom layer of the second cake, bottom side up (so the top of the cake is flat). Frost the top and sides of the cake.

Heat a palette knife or frosting spatula in hot water, shake off any excess water, and use it to smooth the buttercream on the sides and the top of the cake. Continue heating the palette knife and shaking off the excess water, until the buttercream is smooth. (A revolving cake stand will make it easier.) If there is extra buttercream, fill a pastry bag with it to decorate. Garnish with the chocolate espresso beans.

I use skewers and a long, thin flexible knife to cut the cakes evenly.

coffee meringue buttercream

frosts one 9-inch 4-layer cake

Most buttercreams aren't the real thing; they're made from shortening, butter, and flavorings and they're generally pretty awful. Real buttercream is lighter than air and just melts on your tongue. It takes a little time to make but it's so worth it!! If you've never made buttercream, do a practice round and you'll be fine when the pressure is on.

- 2 cups sugar
- 6 extra-large egg whites, at room temperature
- ¼ teaspoon cream of tartar
- Pinch of kosher salt
- 1½ pounds (6 sticks) unsalted butter, at room temperature
- ¼ cup coffee liqueur, such as Kahlúa
- 2 teaspoons pure vanilla extract

Combine the sugar and ⅔ cup of water in a medium heavy-bottomed saucepan, cover, and bring to a boil over high heat. As soon as the sugar dissolves, uncover the pan and place a candy thermometer in the syrup. Cook over high heat until the thermometer registers exactly 240 degrees. (Don't stir!)

Meanwhile, place the egg whites, cream of tartar, and salt in the bowl of an electric mixer fitted with the whisk attachment. Beat the egg whites on high speed until they form stiff peaks.

Carefully pour the syrup into a 2-cup glass measuring cup. With the mixer still on high, very slowly pour the sugar syrup into the egg whites in a thin, steady stream. Leave the mixer on high for about 1 hour (trust me!), until the mixture is completely at room temperature. (If the mixture isn't absolutely at room temperature, the butter will melt and deflate the egg whites!)

With the mixer on medium, add the butter, 2 tablespoons at a time. If the butter starts to melt, stop and wait for the mixture to cool. With the mixer on low, add the coffee liqueur and vanilla. Do not refrigerate; frost the cake while the buttercream is at room temperature.

pecan rum raisin ice cream

makes one quart

Sometimes you just run across a recipe that's simply perfect. I adore rum raisin ice cream and this one based on David Lebovitz's recipe in his book The Perfect Scoop *hits all the right rum and raisin notes with a hint of orange zest. I have to stop myself from making this because when it's in the freezer it calls my name in the middle of the night.*

⅓ cup dark raisins

⅓ cup golden raisins

½ cup dark rum, such as Mount Gay

   3-inch strip of orange zest

1½ cups heavy cream

¾ cup whole milk

1 vanilla bean, split lengthwise

⅔ cup sugar, divided

4 extra-large egg yolks

   Pinch of kosher salt

½ cup pecans, toasted, cooled, and roughly chopped (see note)

The cream mixture is cooked when your finger leaves a trail on the back of a spoon.

To toast pecans, roast them in a 350-degree oven for 5 to 10 minutes, until lightly browned.

Place the dark and golden raisins, rum, and orange zest in a small saucepan. Bring the mixture to a boil over medium heat, remove from the heat, cover, and set aside.

Meanwhile, pour the cream, milk, vanilla bean, and ⅓ cup of the sugar into a large saucepan and heat it to a simmer over medium heat. Place the egg yolks, the remaining ⅓ cup of sugar, and the salt into the bowl of an electric mixer fitted with the paddle attachment and beat on high speed for 3 to 4 minutes, until very thick. When the beater is lifted, the mixture will fall back on itself in a slow ribbon. With the mixer on low, pour ½ cup of the hot cream mixture into the egg mixture. While stirring with a wooden spoon, pour the egg mixture back into the saucepan and cook over medium-low heat, stirring almost constantly, for 8 to 10 minutes, until thickened (175 to 180 degrees on a candy thermometer). The mixture will be thick enough to coat the back of the spoon (see note). Immediately pour the mixture through a fine-mesh sieve, discarding the vanilla bean. Refrigerate for at least 3 hours, until cold.

When ready to freeze, drain the raisin mixture, reserving the rum and discarding the orange zest. Mix 3 tablespoons of the drained rum into the cream mixture (discard the rest). Pour the mixture into an ice cream maker and freeze according to the manufacturer's directions. At the end, stir in the raisins and pecans, transfer to a quart container, and freeze. Because of the alcohol in the rum, the ice cream won't freeze hard; you can scoop it right from the freezer.

chocolate crème brûlée

serves 6

I learned to make crème brûlée from Julia Child's Mastering the Art of French Cooking, *and Jeffrey loved it. It's an elegant "nursery" dessert with its luxuriously creamy center and hard caramelized top. My twist on the classic is to add good Swiss chocolate and a hint of coffee to the custard.*

A kitchen blowtorch isn't as scary as it sounds, and it's better than using the broiler.

- 1 extra-large egg
- 4 extra-large egg yolks
- ½ cup sugar, plus extra for topping
- 3 cups heavy cream
- 8 ounces bittersweet chocolate, such as Lindt, chopped
- 1 teaspoon instant espresso granules
- ¼ cup coffee liqueur, such as Kahlúa
- 1 teaspoon pure vanilla extract

Preheat the oven to 275 degrees. Place six (8-ounce) ramekins in a roasting pan large enough to hold them completely flat.

In a large heatproof bowl, whisk together the egg, egg yolks, and sugar until just combined. Meanwhile, scald the cream in a medium saucepan. Off the heat, add the chocolate and espresso and whisk until the chocolate is melted. Slowly whisk the cream mixture into the egg mixture, then whisk in the coffee liqueur and vanilla. Transfer to a large measuring cup and pour into the prepared ramekins until full.

Place the pan in the oven and carefully pour enough of the hottest tap water into the pan to come halfway up the sides of the ramekins. Bake for 40 to 50 minutes, until the custards are set on the edges but still a little jiggly in the middle when gently shaken. Remove the custards from the water bath, cool to room temperature, wrap in plastic, and refrigerate until firm.

To serve, spread 1 tablespoon of sugar evenly on each custard. With a kitchen blowtorch held one inch from the surface of the crème, heat the sugar until it caramelizes evenly. Allow to cool for 5 minutes and serve.

MAKE AHEAD
The custards can be cooked and refrigerated for 3 days; caramelize before serving.

limoncello ricotta cheesecake

serves 12

I've made this limoncello ricotta cheesecake too many times to count. People can't believe how light and flavorful it is, plus it's nice to have a small square of cheesecake instead of a big rich, dense wedge. Grated lemon zest on top gives it extra flavor and tells people what to expect even before they take a bite.

FOR THE CRUST

Nonstick cooking spray

2 cups graham cracker crumbs (15 crackers)

2 tablespoons sugar

¼ pound (1 stick) unsalted butter, melted

FOR THE FILLING

16 ounces cream cheese, such as Philadelphia, at room temperature

1¼ cups sugar

1½ cups fresh ricotta

½ cup Italian limoncello liqueur, at room temperature

1 teaspoon pure vanilla extract

1 tablespoon grated lemon zest, plus extra for serving (2 lemons)

5 extra-large eggs, at room temperature

A hot dry knife will help make a clean slice.

Preheat the oven to 350 degrees. Position an oven rack in the center of the oven. Spray a 9 × 13 × 2-inch baking pan with nonstick cooking spray.

For the crust, combine the graham cracker crumbs, sugar, and butter in a medium bowl and mix until moistened. Press the mixture evenly in the prepared pan and ¼ inch up the sides. Bake for 8 minutes and set aside to cool.

For the filling, place the cream cheese and sugar in the bowl of an electric mixer fitted with the paddle attachment. Beat on medium speed for 3 minutes, until light and fluffy. Add the ricotta and beat for another minute, scraping down the bowl. With the mixer on low, add the limoncello, vanilla, and lemon zest and beat for one minute. With the mixer on medium-low,

MAKE AHEAD
Prepare completely, wrap, and refrigerate for up to 3 days.

add the eggs, one at a time, beating until incorporated. Scrape down the bowl and mix until the batter is smooth. Pour over the crust.

Place the baking pan in a roasting pan large enough to hold the baking pan completely flat. Place the pan in the oven and carefully pour enough of the hottest tap water into the roasting pan to come halfway up the sides of the baking pan. Bake for 50 to 55 minutes, until almost set in the center. (It will still be a little jiggly when you shake the pan gently.) Turn off the heat and leave the cheesecake in the oven in the water bath for 15 minutes to prevent the cheesecake from cracking. Take the baking pan out of the water bath and place on a rack to cool completely. Wrap the entire pan with plastic wrap and refrigerate for at least 6 hours or overnight. Sprinkle with extra grated lemon zest, cut into 12 pieces, and serve cold.

fresh peach cobbler

serves 6 to 8

I've always made fruit crisps but avoided cobblers because by the time I've prepped the fruit for the filling, the last thing I want to do is start making biscuits for the top. Recently, I came across a topping by Mark Bittman and my version of his drop biscuit topping was the perfect solution. Make this when local peaches are ripe and they'll be easier to peel and so much more flavorful!

4 pounds ripe peaches (8 to 10 large peaches)

¾ cup sugar, plus extra for sprinkling

3 tablespoons cornstarch

½ teaspoon grated orange zest

⅓ cup freshly squeezed orange juice

1 tablespoon unsalted butter

FOR THE TOPPING

1 cup all-purpose flour

¾ cup sugar, plus 2 tablespoons, divided

1 teaspoon baking powder

¾ teaspoon kosher salt

12 tablespoons (1½ sticks) cold unsalted butter, ½-inch-diced

2 extra-large eggs

1 teaspoon pure vanilla extract

¼ teaspoon ground cinnamon

Vanilla ice cream, such as Häagen-Dazs, for serving

Preheat the oven to 350 degrees. Line a sheet pan with parchment paper.

Bring a medium pot of water to a boil. In batches, immerse the peaches for 30 seconds to 3 minutes, testing along the way, until the skins can be peeled off easily with a paring knife. Transfer the peaches to a bowl of ice water to stop the cooking and peel. Large-dice a quarter of the peaches, set aside, and cut the remaining peaches into wedges into a large bowl.

(recipe continues)

In a medium saucepan, whisk together the sugar, cornstarch, orange zest, orange juice, and butter and bring to a boil. Add only the diced peaches (not the wedges), bring back to a boil, then lower the heat and simmer for 3 to 5 minutes, stirring occasionally, until the liquid is thickened and translucent. Mix the cooked peaches with the peach wedges and pour into an 8½ × 11½ × 2-inch oval baking dish and set aside.

For the topping, put the flour, ¾ cup sugar, the baking powder, and salt in the bowl of a food processor fitted with the steel blade and pulse to combine. Add the butter and pulse 15 to 20 times, until it is the size of peas. In a small bowl, beat the eggs and vanilla, and add to the food processor. Pulse just until the mixture is evenly moistened. Spoon dollops of the dough (I use a 1¾-inch ice cream scoop) onto the peaches (it won't cover them all). Combine the remaining 2 tablespoons sugar and the cinnamon and sprinkle on top.

Put the dish on the prepared sheet pan and bake for 50 to 60 minutes, covering loosely with a large sheet of aluminum foil halfway through if the topping is getting too browned. Bake until the topping springs back in the middle when lightly touched. (Both the edge of the crust and the middle should spring back the same way.) Allow to cool for at least 30 minutes and serve warm with the ice cream.

MAKE AHEAD
Prepare the cobbler up to 2 hours before dinner, leave at room temperature, and reheat while you're serving dinner.

spicy hermit bars

makes 14 to 16 bars

This recipe was inspired by one from Martha Stewart and it's just about my favorite bar ever. If you like gingerbread (and I do!), you'll love these!

¼ pound (1 stick) unsalted butter, at room temperature
1 cup light or dark brown sugar, lightly packed
1 extra-large egg, at room temperature
¼ cup unsulphured molasses
2 cups plus 2 tablespoons all-purpose flour
2 teaspoons baking soda
2 teaspoons ground ginger
1½ teaspoons ground cinnamon
1½ teaspoons ground cloves
½ teaspoon kosher salt
½ cup golden raisins
⅓ cup minced crystallized ginger (not in syrup)
1 cup sifted confectioners' sugar
Dark rum, such as Mount Gay
Grated lemon zest

Preheat the oven to 375 degrees. Line a sheet pan with parchment paper.

Place the butter and brown sugar in the bowl of an electric mixer fitted with the paddle attachment and beat on medium speed for 2 minutes, until light and fluffy. With the mixer on low, add the egg, scrape down the bowl, then mix in the molasses.

Sift together the flour, baking soda, ground ginger, cinnamon, cloves, and salt. With the mixer on low, slowly add the dry ingredients to the butter mixture, mixing just until combined. Mix in the raisins and crystallized ginger. Cover the bowl with plastic wrap and refrigerate for 30 minutes.

Turn the dough out onto a very lightly floured board, form it into a disk with lightly floured hands, and cut it in half. Roll each half into a log 12 inches long and place them 3 inches apart on

MAKE AHEAD
Prepare the bars, cool completely, wrap well, and refrigerate. Serve at room temperature.

the prepared sheet pan. Bake for 20 minutes; the logs will still be soft in the center.

Meanwhile, whisk the confectioners' sugar with 5 to 6 teaspoons rum to make a pourable glaze. While the logs are still warm, drizzle the glaze back and forth across the logs with a teaspoon and sprinkle them with the lemon zest. Allow to cool. Cut each log crosswise into 1½-inch-wide bars.

frozen hot chocolate

serves 4

Serendipity 3 is an iconic New York restaurant on East 60th Street. Jeffrey took me there on a date during the Thanksgiving holiday from college so many years ago. They are famous for their frozen hot chocolate, which is beyond decadent. This is my homage to that treat.

After testing many chocolates, I prefer Lindt bittersweet chocolate.

    4 ounces bittersweet chocolate, such as Lindt
    1½ tablespoons unsweetened cocoa powder, such as
        Pernigotti
    1½ tablespoons sugar
    ½ cup half-and-half
    1½ cups whole milk
    4 tablespoons coffee liqueur, such as Kahlúa, or brewed
        espresso
    1 teaspoon pure vanilla extract
    4 cups ice
        Sweetened Whipped Cream, for serving (page 213)
        Grated bittersweet chocolate, for garnish
        Straws, for serving

Break the bittersweet chocolate into pieces and place it in a medium bowl set over a pot of simmering water, stirring occasionally, until just melted. Off the heat, whisk in the cocoa powder, sugar, and half-and-half and set aside.

Place ¾ cup of the milk, 2 tablespoons of the coffee liqueur, ½ teaspoon of the vanilla, and half of the chocolate mixture in a blender. Add 2 cups of the ice and blend for several minutes, until the mixture is thick but not icy, like a frozen daiquiri. (You can add a little more milk or ice if it's too thick or too thin.) Pour into two (10-ounce) ice cream soda glasses and top each with a generous dollop of whipped cream and some grated chocolate. Repeat for the second two glasses. Serve ice cold with straws and long-handled spoons.

Roast Chicken with Bread & Arugula Salad
Make It Ahead

Jeffrey's all-time favorite dinners

Perfect Roast Chicken
The Barefoot Contessa Cookbook

Parmesan Chicken
Family Style

Indonesian Ginger Chicken
The Barefoot Contessa Cookbook

Crispy Mustard-Roasted Chicken
Foolproof

Roast Chicken with Bread & Arugula Salad
Make It Ahead

Summer Filet of Beef with Béarnaise Mayonnaise
Make It Ahead

Steakhouse Steaks with Roquefort Chive Butter
How Easy Is That?

Herb-Roasted Fish
Make It Ahead

Mustard-Roasted Fish
Back to Basics

Slow-Roasted Spiced Pork
Make It Ahead

Scallops Provençal
Barefoot in Paris

Weeknight Bolognese
How Easy Is That?

resources

ina's pantry

ina's starter kitchen

ina's professional
kitchen

ina's pantry

For sources, please go to BarefootContessa.com.

Nielsen-Massey vanilla

Olio Santo olive oil

Tellicherry black peppercorns

Diamond Crystal kosher salt

Fleur de sel

Maldon flaked sea salt

Good vinegars

Hellmann's mayonnaise

Texmati rices

Maille whole-grain Dijon mustard

De Cecco pasta

Grey Poupon Dijon mustard

Pernigotti cocoa powder

Nestlé's semisweet chocolate morsels and chocolate chunks

Lindt bittersweet chocolate

Urbani or D'Artagnan white truffle butter

ina's starter kitchen

For sources, please go to BarefootContessa.com.

Stainless-steel mixing bowls

4 knives: paring, 8- or 10-inch
    chef's knife, slicing knife, and
    serrated knife

Sheet pans (half sheet pans)

Restaurant supply cookware

Electric hand mixer

Zester

Oven thermometer

Cast-iron skillets

Glass and metal measuring cups

Stainless-steel box grater

Candy thermometer

Kitchen timers

Reamer for juicing citrus fruit

Assorted baking pans

Assorted muffin pans

Assorted cooking utensils,
    such as rubber spatulas and
    stainless-steel spoons

ina's professional kitchen

For sources, please go to BarefootContessa.com.

All-Clad cookware

10- and 12-inch All-Clad sauté pans

16- to 20-quart stockpot

Le Creuset Dutch ovens

Food mill

KitchenAid 4.5-quart electric mixer

Cuisinart Pro Custom 11 food
    processor

Good knives and knife block

Kitchen scale

Oven-to-table baking dishes

Mini food chopper

Set of glass mixing bowls

Electric juicer

Knife sharpener

French rolling pin

Stretch-Tite plastic wrap

index

recipe index